God Bless!

Please, God, Let Them Be Amazing

PLEASE, GOD,
LET THEM BE AMAZING

One Ordinary Family,
Two Extraordinary Miracles

KYLE DEREK ERVIN

TWO HARBORS PRESS

Two Harbors Press
212 3rd Avenue North, Suite 290
Minneapolis, MN 55401
612.455.2293
www.TwoHarborsPress.com

ISBN-13: 978-1-938690-01-3
LCCN: 2012941378

Distributed by Itasca Books

Cover Design by Sophie Chi
Typeset by Madge Duffy

Printed in the United States of America

To the tireless staffs of
Anaheim Regional Medical Center
and Mission Hospital of Mission Viejo,
who do God's work every day.

CONTENTS

PROLOGUE

There is a strange reality about days that change the rest of your life. They usually start off the same as any other day. My life changed on a Wednesday—a Wednesday that was supposed to be a day of relief, a day of celebration. My wife and I had a new son.

Instead of a day of relief and celebration, I found a day of horror and a grief so deep and black that, at the time, I could not imagine a way out of it.

CHAPTER ONE
Relentless Waves

August 2009

The vision of a tiny casket slowly lowered into the ground crowded out every thought. I tried to push it away, tried to think of something else, but I could not. Fear, now my constant companion, had again taken control of my mind, raising my heart rate, shortening my breath. I glanced in the rearview mirror ensuring that all of my three children—Grace, age seven; Isaiah, age four; and my two-year-old Noah—were sleeping before I gave voice to Fear.

"What if this baby dies?" I asked my wife, who sat in the passenger seat of our minivan.

"Little ears," my wife reminded me, in the code we had worked out over eight years of marriage, that one of our children might be listening. She shifted in her seat, maneuvering around her pregnant belly to check on them.

"They're asleep," I said, peering into the rearview mirror again to make sure that they were, in fact, still sleeping.

I drove north on Interstate 5. The hills of Camp Pendleton Marine Corps Base rolled east to our right, and the setting sun fell into the Pacific Ocean on our left. We were on our way home from San Diego where we had taken a weekend trip to the zoo in hopes of finding some relief from the horror our life had become. Fear had moved in with us, and we had been desperate to get away.

"It's cold." She turned off the air vent on her side of the car.

"This sun is baking me." I adjusted my own vent up onto my face. "We need to think about this."

"You're right. Better now than after. It's just..." Tears gathered in her eyes as she rubbed her belly.

"I know." I reached across the center console and grabbed her hand. I took my gaze from the road for a moment and looked into her hazel-green eyes.

She fought to keep tears back but failed. "I don't want a lot of people. I don't think I could handle a big deal."

"Honey, if he dies, it's going to be a big deal. I'm not sure we can do anything about that."

"Poppi wouldn't be able to do it."

I imagined my father-in-law in his deacon's robes, standing over the tiny coffin, trying to get through the burial rite. I blinked away the water that came to my eyes at the thought.

"No, you're right. He couldn't bury his grandson." I thought about our options. "If Father Martin were here..."

"Yeah. What about Father Brian?"

"That's a good idea."

"This sucks."

"Yep."

"I'm glad I have you." She gripped my hand harder, signaling me to look at her. In her eyes was the truth of her words, and I could not help but be glad that we had each other to go through this.

"Me too," I replied.

"I couldn't do this without you."

"Me neither." We continued north in silence, the hum of wheels on the road the only sound accompanying our thoughts. My mind drifted back over the past six months and found a jumbled series of vignettes—portraits of the some of the pleasures and trials the two of us had already faced together.

***

June 2009 (Two months earlier)

"And if it's a boy?" my wife, Brynn, asked me. She ran her fingers through her hair, peering into the bathroom mirror. "I need to dye my hair," she said, noting that the auburn color was showing the gray at the roots.

"You should just let it go gray. What do you think about Anthony?"

"I can't let it go gray. I'm only thirty-four … Anthony?"

"Yeah, Anthony."

"I like it."

I knew she would like it. She's the Catholic in the family, and I didn't figure she would have a problem naming one of her kids after a saint.

As for me, it seemed only natural to name our son after the saint that helps me on an almost daily basis. Although I am not Catholic, I regularly utilize the services of St. Anthony of Padua—the patron saint of lost things.

As the poster child of attention deficit disorder, I have a tendency to put down very important things in places that seem perfectly reasonable at the time. However, when it comes time to use those things, I can't remember where I put them.

"Have you seen my wallet?"

"No. Did you pray to St. Anthony?"

"Not yet."

"Weeeelll…"

3

St. Anthony doesn't seem to care that I'm not Catholic. He helps me find all the junk I am constantly misplacing. For that help, I am incredibly grateful.

August 2009

The car tires rattled on the reflectors as I changed lanes. *A name—this baby has a name. His name is Anthony. And he is a blessing we never intended.*

Only months earlier, it had been something of a joke that my wife and I were going to have a fourth child. The joke began in April 2009, as the mess in my garage had finally exceeded my considerable tolerance for messiness. I spent two full days cleaning out the garage and, in doing that, I took ALL of our old baby clothes and toys and my wife's collection of maternity clothes to Goodwill—ALL OF THEM.

Brynn and I already had three children, and we were *done* with having babies. God had another idea. Exactly four days later, Brynn found out she was pregnant.

Not only were we distressed by the daunting prospect of a fourth child but, unfortunately, this would also turn out to be the toughest pregnancy Brynn ever experienced.

Her troubles started a couple of weeks in, when she started having morning sickness. Brynn had dealt with morning sickness before, but this time it was different.

"Get me a bag."

"You gotta puke?"

"Yep."

We were on a road trip coming back from Big Bear Lake. Brynn was driving to avoid motion sickness. The sickness still came. I grabbed one of the plastic grocery bags we had stashed on the floorboard of the van and handed it to her.

"Grab the wheel," she said.

The road had no shoulder and we could not pull

over. I took the steering wheel in my left hand, trying to keep the van inside the winding lane, driving from the passenger seat.

Brynn worked the gas and the brakes as she puked, her eyes just peaking over the plastic bag catching the mess so that she could see the road ahead.

"Morning" sickness didn't begin to describe what she was going through. What she had was "all-day" sickness. Any time she ate anything, it was bound to come back up about fifteen or twenty minutes later. She started to only eat foods that tasted good on the way down *and* on the way back up... Bananas were safe. Any kind of nut was not.

Rather than gaining weight, as she did with all three previous pregnancies, she was losing weight. Initially the doctor was not overly concerned, but as the months wore on, the concern grew.

Though Brynn had never taken even an aspirin during her previous pregnancies, she began to take an anti-nausea medication just so she could keep some food down. It did not work too well, but it did provide some relief.

Then, about five months into the pregnancy, just as Brynn's nausea was starting to abate somewhat, we received a letter in the mail. It was addressed to Brynn and came from the UC Irvine Genetic Counseling Program.

That's how we found out that our unborn child had tested positive on a screening test for genetic disorders. No phone call, no personal conversation with someone who might explain—we were blindsided by a letter. And we were terrified.

That was the day that Fear came to live with me. He didn't just stop by for the afternoon like he does when I hear the screeching of car tires, or when the plane I'm in hits heavy turbulence. He walked into my home, crawled up on my chest, wrapped his arms around me like an invisible giant anaconda, and squeezed.

At first, the squeezing was slight. *It'll go away,* I thought. But as time went on, the squeezing got worse. I found myself taking in deep breaths for no apparent reason, just trying to get enough air. Fear, I learned, is a suffocating monster.

Along with Fear came guilt. I felt guilty for being afraid. I felt guilty because I was not sure of what I was more afraid of—that he might die, or that he might live and have terrible things wrong with him and need extraordinary care for his entire life. And in that guilt, Fear bathed.

My skin was no barrier. From my chest, he moved into my gut. There he sat, all day, stealing my appetite and driving my mind to dark thoughts—thoughts that filled my days with shadows and kept me awake at night, whispering in my ear. I would lie in bed and listen because I had no choice. Then I'd get up, go out to the living room, and turn on the computer.

I tried to tame the fear with knowledge, losing myself in terminology. My mind grappled to understand new words, such as alpha-fetoprotein, amniocentesis, human chorionic gonadotropin, trisomy 18, trisomy 21, myelomeningocele. But my newfound knowledge only served to reinforce Fear.

Trisomy 18: Edward's syndrome. Nearly always fatal in the first year of life.

Trisomy 21: Down's syndrome.

Myelomeningocele: A serious and common form of spina bifida.

***

I drove up the freeway and these new words rolled through my head, bouncing through my brain like bullets. One of the words I learned—amniocentesis—did not bounce, it exploded in my mind. I tried to take in a breath, as Fear, again, tightened around my chest.

***

"An amnio is the only way you will know for certain if the child has a genetic disorder." A physician spoke to us in a shockingly sparse office. The office did not look as if it belonged to anyone. There was a desk with a computer monitor, and two chairs for us to sit in, but there was nothing to identify that a person worked there on a day-to-day basis. No pictures or personal effects of any kind. It was a place where people received bad news and, as such, it was not a suitable place for someone to work day in and day out.

Initially, we had decided not to do the amnio. We knew it would require sticking a very large needle into my wife's belly to retrieve some of the amniotic fluid. Yes, it was the only way to be certain of genetic abnormalities, but the procedure also carried the risk of accidently terminating the pregnancy. This was an unacceptable risk for my Catholic wife.

I wanted to know though. I needed to know what I was in for, but I would not try to convince her... *her body, her decision. I must deal with whatever she decides and support her. That's my job here.*

After she had decided, however, Brynn got some advice from a friend with a special needs child.

"Brynn, you need to be prepared. The more you know, the better you'll be able to care for the baby. If your baby needs some kind of specialist within hours of being born, you need to know that."

Thirty-four years of Catholic upbringing is hard to get past, and Brynn still struggled with the idea. That was until Father Eugene, a very close friend of her family, gave her another piece of advice. "Brynn, God knows your intent. He knows you are trying to do what is right for the baby."

Less than two weeks later, I was holding my wife's hand. She was lying on an exam table and the doctor ran the ultrasound wand over her round belly.

Anthony's black-and-white skeletal image showed on the screen as it had many times in the past few weeks. We had become intimately familiar with the ultrasound because, beyond the possibility of genetic disorders, Anthony was also not growing at the rate he should have been.

This time, the ultrasound was different. This time they were using it to guide a three-inch needle into Brynn's belly. The needle was clearly visible on the screen as it pushed and then punctured her skin. She gripped my hand hard as it went through her uterine wall, and she continued to squeeze until the needle was finally removed.

It would take ten days to get the results.

In the ten days we waited, Fear broke over us like the relentless waves of an angry ocean, nearly drowning us. We struggled to keep our heads above it, barely able to get a free breath, only to be pounded with another wave that sent us back under. In an effort to breathe, we decided to make the trip to San Diego. We planned our child's funeral on that car ride home.

CHAPTER TWO
My Best Friend's Sister

San Diego State University, 1995

"My sister's coming this Friday and bringing her friend," my roommate, Joshua Dowell, told me. At the time, we lived together with two other roommates, John Suarez and Tommy Vice, in a well-used college area rental house. It was the prototypical bachelor pad. The rent was relatively cheap and, when you included the one-car garage as an additional bedroom (where my roommate Tommy froze in the winter and cooked in the summer), it had plenty of room for four grown men, and even the occasional houseguest.

Perched atop one of the many ravines surrounding the San Diego State University College area, the back-yard was large. It ran about forty or fifty yards back before hitting the property line, providing ample room for the occasional kegger. Then after the property line, there was just the dropping ravine.

The slope of the backyard was terraced into three levels. The highest terrace was level to the back of the house and covered by a concrete patio. Smack in the middle of the patio was an old washing machine drum converted to a fire pit. And for some reason, sitting right there on the patio, a little ways from the fire pit, nestled up against the fence, was a random old toilet.

On the second terrace was a large trampoline right

next to a large tool shed. The height of the shed was such that the roof butted right up against the deck. We placed two folding chairs atop it. There we sat, drank beer, smoked cigars, and solved all the world's problems. Of course, because that shed was next to the trampoline, we decided it was the perfect launching point to jump onto the trampoline—a source of several injuries while we lived there but, miraculously, no deaths.

The third terrace was dominated by a large pine tree with a three-inch bed of pine needles at the base. The only times we went down there were to place our "long distance" BB gun targets, or to cut through to the ravine where we hiked when we were ridiculously drunk.

The entire yard was covered in weeds. Beneath the weeds were hundreds of broken beer bottles and crushed beer cans that were the result of our many BB gun target matches, and our habit of chucking recently consumed beers down into the yard.

The inside of the house was not much of an improvement over the outside. On the fridge was a white board that had been put up for notes, but had mostly been used to count all the mice we killed with our BB guns. Field mice came up from the canyon and made quite a comfy home in our walls. And why should we buy mouse traps or tell the landlord to hire an exterminator when we had BB guns? Yeah, we didn't see any reason either.

"There he goes! Get him." BBs fired, then ricocheted throughout the house.

"He went under the stove."

"Turn on the stove." We waited, with our BB guns poised and ready to fire.

"Oh shit! There he goes! Get him! Get him!"

"Got him! That one's mine."

"Go put it on the board."

Inside the fridge you'd have been hard-pressed to

find edible food. You were almost guaranteed to find beer and something resembling a Chia Pet. In the sink were more Chia Pets growing on the dishes piled there.

The couches and the carpet were masterpieces, a la Jackson Pollock, of beer, spaghetti sauce, and Top Ramen stains. Every countertop was covered in a layer of dust. On the living room wall there was a massive mural in black spray paint, depicting all four occupants of the house. It was painted by a friend of our roommate, Tommy, as payment for allowing him and some other guys a place to sleep for a couple of nights.

As such, there were generally only two occasions for which this house was ever cleaned. 1) One of our parents was going to visit, or 2) One of us was going to have a girl over. Josh's news fell into this second category, and motivated us to get the place cleaned up—*mostly.* At the very least, we vacuumed, washed the dishes, wiped up the dust, and scrubbed the toilet seats.

As Friday came, my excitement grew. I was young and single and definitely "looking." I approached every opportunity to meet a girl with equal parts optimism, curiosity, and lust. In this heightened state, my willpower was tested as I tried to stay in the back of the house when I heard the front door open upon Josh's return from the train station where he had gone to pick up the girls.

Josh brought them inside, and I was not disappointed. Here, ready to stay the entire weekend at *our* house, were two beautiful young women. Josh's sister, Brynn, had a girl-next-door face, hazel eyes accentuated by her dark brows and eyelashes, long dark hair, and even longer legs. The other beauty, a little bit shorter than Brynn, with sandy blonde hair and green eyes, was her best friend, Phaidra.

If I were not already drinking before they got there, I was certainly drinking as soon as the introductions were over. Their beauty was intimidating, and liquid courage was going to be needed.

We decided to pull out all the stops and treat the girls to one of the treasures of the San Diego State College area. As a group we walked down to Los Panchos.

The smell of warm tortillas and carne asada, and copious amounts of guacamole wafted through the air as we approached the blue-and-white A-frame building of the once-upon-a-time Wienerschnitzel. We all ordered, sat on the patio, and ate, enjoying the mingled sensations of a cool ocean breeze mixed with the warmth of the evening sun.

Stuffed to bursting on Mexican food, we walked back to our house where we started a fire in the fire pit and went to work on the beer ration for the weekend. A few beers in, and everyone was primed for some trampoline time. We all went down to the middle terrace and got on the trampoline. We laughed ourselves silly as we flew through the air.

Soon we all were breathing heavily, and so caught our breath by way of more drinking—then more trampoline time, punctuated by more drinking, and so on, until we were all incredibly exhausted, and very drunk. By this time, the spring sun found its way beneath the horizon and we gathered around the fire, drinking more and enjoying each other's company.

Then it happened. One by one, my roommates and, finally, Phaidra went off to sleep. Brynn and I were the last two awake. I could not believe my good fortune. After all that anticipation, the night was ending exactly as I had hoped. I was alone with a beautiful girl.

It was getting late and Brynn was chilled, despite the fire, so we moved the party indoors and made ourselves comfortable on the couch by the mural. I sat about a foot away from her, having that awful internal debate, *Should I try to kiss her?*

I was twenty years old, and hopeful and eager to move this burgeoning relationship into the physical realm. But it was not to happen that night. Instead, the two of us experienced one of those magical evenings that happens so seldom in a life. We sat together on the dirty, stained couch, less than a foot separating us, and talked—all night long.

She told me how she and Josh had grown up together. Their families were very close and so they grew up calling each other brother and sister. We talked about our parents, our sisters, God and religion, boyfriends and girlfriends. By the time four a.m. rolled around, it was apparent that there was powerful chemistry between us. But there were also walls between us. She had a boyfriend, *and* she was Josh's "sister." So, although neither of us wanted to, we tore ourselves from each other and went to bed.

The next day, my sister Alisa was moving apartments, and I had promised to help. I drove two hours north to Riverside to fulfill that promise. I spent most of the day moving furniture and boxes and chasing her very pissed-off cat around the apartment, and the only thought in my mind was getting it all done as fast as I could so that I might be able to get back to San Diego, to the beautiful girl I had just spent all night talking with.

Brynn Holderness, Phaidra Speirs,
Odessa Speirs, Katie Holderness

CHAPTER THREE
Marooned

August 2009

Days after our attempt to escape Fear, the results from the amniocentesis came back. They were negative for genetic defects.

For ten days, Fear had been trying to drown us. Those results were a lifesaver. We held on tight and, finally, we were able to breathe. We rejoiced in the news for several days, but our respite was temporary. Fear, it seems, came to like our house, and was soon comfortable again.

We came to find that the baby was still not growing at the rate he should have been. The diagnosis was intrauterine growth restriction (IUGR). More terminology, more acronyms, more research, more Fear.

Increased risk of fetal death.

Non-reassuring fetal heart rate.

Increased risk for hypoxia (lack of oxygen).

Increased risk for motor and neurological disabilities.

Brynn was put on bedrest by her doctor. Though she was frustrated by her inability to do very much, the break from her job as a third grade teacher was a welcome rest. Furthermore, so long as we put her in a wheelchair, she could still go to our kids' soccer games and make the occasional trip to Disneyland. For a time, Brynn got to play at being the stay-at-home mom we had always wanted for her to be.

Initially, Anthony's growth rate responded well to Brynn's decreased stress. He showed several weeks of good growth. However, after about four or five weeks, his growth was again below par. In addition, Brynn's amniotic fluid was low. She was admitted to Anaheim Regional Medical Center, on November 17, and placed on total bedrest.

Anaheim Regional Medical Center is, on the surface, an entirely unremarkable hospital. Like hundreds or even thousands of hospitals throughout the country, it goes about its daily business anonymously. It quietly watches over the health of the residents of Orange County with little recognition of the fact.

Like so many others, I thought nothing of Anaheim Regional as I walked through the doors the day my wife was admitted. It was a place to have a baby. That was all. It would turn out to be so much more.

***

"God, I want to get out of here!" Brynn told me, just about every time I visited.

I tried to cheer her up. "What do you mean? You've got the Hallmark Channel, *and* it's Thanksgiving. You get to watch *all* the cheesy Christmas movies you can handle!"

My wife *loves* the holidays. From September to January, she fills our home with decorations. In September, she starts modestly, with a smattering of back-to-school stuff. As a teacher, she has numerous little red school houses and carved wooden apples. She puts them all out and garnishes their appearance with gourds, and leaves, and other fall stuff.

For Halloween she raises the intensity a bit, putting window stickers on the front window, ghosts and witches in our garden, and pumpkins all over our front yard. As Thanksgiving rolls around, she brings out some turkeys and cornucopias, but by that point, she's already looking ahead to December—the month in which she really loses her mind.

The moment Thanksgiving dinner is put away, my wife begins to pull out the Christmas music CDs, or puts on a cheesy Christmas movie (she *loves* cheesy Christmas movies) and gets busy converting our house into the North Pole.

Unfortunately, when she was in the hospital, all the cheesy Christmas movies she could handle were not enough to cheer her up. And, though I purchased a big plastic turkey poster and various sundry decorations for her hospital room, the downside of total bedrest in the hospital still outweighed the benefits.

Brynn was stranded in a thirty-six by eighty-inch hospital bed. Wrapped to her pregnant belly, with elastic straps, were a contraction monitor and a fetal heart rate monitor. They were on so tight that they left bright-red indentations in her skin. At night, she had to wear cuffs around her legs that inflated and deflated constantly in an effort to prevent blood clots from forming in her inactive legs. They kept her awake all night long.

On top of all this, due to the H1N1 virus scare that was going on at the time, no children under sixteen were allowed in the hospital. As any mother will understand, this was an impossible situation for my wife. She was essentially marooned from her family. Her desert island was her hospital room.

Brynn's isolation was only compounded by the fact that she was admitted the day before our oldest son, Isaiah's, birthday on November 18th. The weekend after Thanksgiving, he was to have his "big" five-year-old birthday party at a place called Pump-It-Up. She was not able to be there.

I bought her a laptop at one of the Black Friday sales the day after Thanksgiving, and took my work laptop with me to the party, and we Skyped the whole event. But I think that just made it worse for Brynn. There, on the computer screen, her eyes glistened as her son sat on the big inflatable throne with a crown on his head and opened up all his gifts.

On the brighter side, being the only long-term patient in Labor and Delivery gave Brynn the opportunity to chat with the staff who cared for her. Never one to allow her own discomfort to get in the way of making new friends, Brynn got to know many of them very well.

A couple weeks in, Brynn's new friends in Labor and Delivery decided they could not let her suffer any longer. Two of them came to me, devilish smiles on their faces, and told me of their plan to sneak in the children to visit their mom. It was very cloak and dagger. One of the nurses would take a "smoke break" and leave open a back entrance. I would then sneak the kids in through the back entrance, and take them straight to Labor and Delivery.

The Ervins, November 2009

Their plan went off perfectly. It was a short visit, but I thank God for those nurses that bent the rules to get the kids in there, because as it turned out, it would be more than a month before they would see their mother again, and when they did, she would not recognize any of them.

Despite the total bedrest, Brynn's amniotic fluid got lower. She was having preterm contractions that the baby was not tolerating very well. Our whole family spent two weeks listening to the *swish, swish, swish* of his heart and staring at the screen of the fetal heart-rate monitor, terrified every time his rhythm dropped that it would not return to normal.

The doctors were in a terrible spot. Should they leave the baby in utero, there was the risk that one of Brynn's contractions could stress him so much that his heart could stop entirely. On the other hand, if they were to deliver him too early, he could succumb to the many complications inherent with premature birth.

On two occasions I donned the disposable scrubs, paper booties, and face mask in preparation for a C-section, only to be told that we were going to hold off a little longer. The second time this happened, Brynn had fasted all day in preparation for the surgery. I was in her room, trying to get the elastic at the cuff of the scrubs over my shoes when a perinatologist we had never met before came into Brynn's room.

He was a self-assured Indian man who had perfected the art of professional detachment. Every movement, every word, every facial expression was calculated to project confidence in his abilities. He wore sunglasses and my first impression was, *what a cocky bastard*.

"I apologize for the sunglasses," was the first thing he said. "I just had my eyes dilated."

Sunglasses or no, he still seemed like a pretty cocky fellow to me. He looked at her chart, and did some calculations, and then told Brynn and me that they would not be doing the C-section that day. "We need to wait a little longer," he said matter-of-factly. He was not prepared for Brynn's response.

"You've got to be fucking kidding me!"

Yes, my wife is a very sweet lady. But when she's upset, she could make a truck driver blush. She went on. "I've been fasting all day! I'm done! I want this to be done! I need to get the hell out..." her last sentence trailed off as her words tumbled into raw emotion.

Oh shit, I thought as I tried to calm and comfort Brynn. I was mentally preparing for the verbal combat I was about to have with this doctor I had never met before, when I saw something amazing. Under Brynn's barrage of foul language, his carefully sculpted image of professional detachment crumbled, revealing that which doctors may often feel, but rarely reveal—compassion.

"I understand that you are upset. But I also know that you want to do what is best for this baby, and we need to let him cook a little longer. The longer he stays inside, the better his chances when he's born. If we can keep him in there for one more week..." he explained.

Brynn did not respond. Her thoughts on "one more week" were written all over her face. Eventually, though, she nodded her head and waited for the doctor to leave.

The physician's name was Dr. Wigi, and he would come to be another of Brynn's friends within the walls of Anaheim Memorial. And though he was not required to do so, he made certain he was on hand when it came time to deliver Anthony.

As it happened, Brynn did not have to wait the entire week. Only a couple of days after her outburst with Dr. Wigi, after only thirty-five weeks of pregnancy, and a little over two weeks of being poked and prodded and restricted to a bed in a noisy hospital, and eating crappy hospital food, the doctors were not willing to hold off any longer. The ultrasound showed that Brynn's amniotic fluid was down to zero. It was time for us to have a baby.

The decision had finally been made but the C-section room was being used, so we had to wait until the room and the doctors were available. Unfortunately, the baby's reactions to contractions worsened, and we had several instances in which we could not find his heart rate at all. Fear and tension filled the room like a billowing cloud of noxious gas, suffocating me again.

We moved the heart rate monitor over her belly, added more gel, moved it again, desperately trying to find the *swish, swish, swish* of his heart. My own heart ripped through my chest. All we found was silence—a reprieve—a few heartbeats swishing. Then it was gone again. Finally, the nurse, now almost as frantic as we were, decided to whisk Brynn off for surgery prep.

I donned my disposable surgical scrubs, white paper booties, and funny paper hat, and waited in the hallway.

In the movies, emergency surgeries happen so quickly. They run the patient down the hallway on a gurney, and suddenly they are in surgery. In reality you have to wait for things like anesthesia to take effect. I sat there, elbows on my knees, noticing how my knuckles turned white as I interlocked my fingers and tried to squeeze Fear away.

When Brynn was finally ready for surgery, they wheeled her in and I followed. The anesthesiologist sat above her head, wearing a plastic face shield over a surgical mask. Even behind the mask, Brynn could tell who it was.

"Hey, is that Dr. Wu?"

"Yes, it is," he said in his thickly accented English.

"Kyle, this is Dr. Wu. He gave me all of my IVs."

Dr. Wu had given Brynn all of her IVs during her bed-rest after one of the nurses blew out Brynn's vein and she ended up with phlebitis. Dr. Wu was another doctor Brynn had charmed.

"Nice to meet you," I said.

"We're finally going to have this baby!" she said to him, her ever-present charm always on display.

"Congratulations," he replied.

A visual barrier was placed at her chest, so she could not see them cutting into her stomach, and on the other side of the barrier were Dr. Hernandez and Dr. Wigi, both ready to deliver Anthony.

They did an amazing job. The entire procedure took maybe twenty minutes. It was as uneventful as the pregnancy was eventful. Anthony Alan Ervin came into the world on Tuesday, December 1, 2009. Brynn and I were utterly relieved to hear his cry fill the operating room.

Yes, he was very small (he weighed only two pounds, twelve ounces, and measured only 15 ¾ inches long) and he would be in the neonatal intensive care unit (or NICU) for quite some time. But he was alive and strong enough to cry. He had a fighting chance. Finally, it was time for Fear to leave my house.

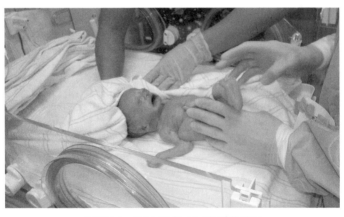

Anthony Alan Ervin on His Birthday

"You have to baptize him," Brynn reminded me. Her father, Alan, a deacon of the Catholic Church, taught me how to give him an emergency baptism in case he did not live long enough for the real deal. In the operating room, they had small vials of sterile water, and they gave me some. "I baptize you in the name of the Father and the Son and the Holy Spirit, Amen."

I cut his chord; they performed the Apgar tests and took him to the NICU.

Tuesday was the eventful day. It was the most traumatic and exciting delivery Brynn and I had experienced of all four of our children. It was to be the only delivery that Brynn would never remember.

CHAPTER FOUR

The Best Day of My Life

Marine Corps Recruit Depot, San Diego California, 1995

Only a couple of months after meeting Brynn for the very first time, I found myself standing on yellow footprints that had been painted onto the concrete. A man was screaming at me. "Hold your arms out in front of you! Aye aye, sir!" he finished each sentence with the expected reply.

Fifty young men shouted in unison, "AYE AYE, SIR!" and held their arms out in front of them.

"Make a fist! Aye aye, sir!"

"AYE AYE, SIR!"

"Hold your thumb straight along your fist like this! Aye aye, sir!"

"AYE AYE, SIR!"

"Now hold your arms straight down along your sides! Aye aye, sir!"

"AYE AYE, SIR!"

"Your heels are together. Your feet are at a forty-five-degree angle! Aye aye, sir!"

"AYE AYE, SIR!"

"You are now standing at the position of attention! This is the only position in which you will address any Marine! Is that understood?"

"YES, SIR!"

I was at Marine Corps Recruit Depot (MCRD) San

Diego. It was the first day of basic training, otherwise known as boot camp. It was the first day of three months of hell.

Only a few weeks earlier, I had no intention of joining the Marines. I was actually enrolled for the summer at Miramar Junior College where I had planned to get my Emergency Medical Technician Certificate. I was doing this because, at the time, I wanted to become a firefighter.

Even fifteen years later, it's difficult to explain why I ended up joining. I think, in the end, it was a stew pot of reasons—patriotism, the challenge, boredom with the state of my life at the time, all mixed together and seasoned with my fear of being "predictable." I never even considered the fact that chicks dig a guy in uniform—honest.

Whatever the reasons for my decision, once I had made it, I went all out. I have always been rather decisive. Many of my former teachers and principals might call it "impulsive." Either way, less than a month later, I was packing my bags and headed off to MCRD.

Now, I had seen movies, so I figured I was prepared for what was in store. Guys were going to be yelling at me. *So what?* Thanks to my impulsiveness, I've had people (teachers, principals, parents) yelling at me my entire life. I was going to have to work out a lot. *So what?* I've been playing competitive soccer my entire life. I've been through double days and Coopers Test and done my fair share of sit-ups. There was even a part of me that relished the thought of how fit I was going to get. I was ready for whatever they were going to throw at me.

No, I wasn't.

From the yellow footprints, we were ushered into a room of red bins. We were being yelled at constantly. "Shut your goddamn cock holsters! You will sit down, Indian style, with your left foot over your right foot! Put your left hand on your left knee, and your right hand on your right knee!"

These men that were yelling, they were not just angry. They yelled at me as if I were the dog that crapped on their lawn. Every word they spoke dripped with condescension. To them, I was filth. No, I was less than filth. I was "unsatisfactory."

The red bins were for sorting, and I couldn't say what went into which bag, but by the end, every item that had come with me was stowed away in its proper place. After that, it was time for haircuts.

There were several barbers' chairs. The electric clippers buzzed, and pounds of hair fell at the barbers' feet. Some guys had their heads shaved already, but the barbers didn't care. They scraped the clippers across their heads, too.

I can remember one guy had a bulldog tattoo with the letters USMC freshly inked on his arm. When one of the drill instructors caught site of it, he went insane. "Who the fuck do you think you are? You are not a fucking Marine, recruit! You do not rate this tattoo!"

He took a black marker and started coloring over the brand new and likely very painful tattoo. "If I see this tattoo again before graduation day, I will personally rip off your head and shit down your throat! Do you understand me?"

"Yes, sir!" The recruit grimaced at the pain in his arm.

Thankful that I hadn't already shaved my head, or gotten a premature USMC tattoo, I plopped into the chair for the quickest, most painful haircut I ever had. The teeth of the clippers bit into my scalp, yanking my curly hair, and cutting it within millimeters of my scull at the same time.

Having your head shaved is a psychological cliff, a point of no return. I rubbed my hands over my head, and knew I had stepped in a deep pile of shit, and the only way out was to walk through it to the other side.

My first introduction to "the way things get done in the Marine Corps" was in my first week, while I was still in Receiving Battalion. Our platoon had strict orders to not use the restroom (heretofore to be known as the head) until later that morning when we would have to take a piss test for drugs. One of my fellow recruits couldn't wait and so asked for permission to use the head. "Sir. This recruit requests permission to use the head!" At MCRD recruits are forbidden to use the pronoun "I."

The drill instructor went ballistic. "Listen, shithole! If you can't piss in that cup when it comes time, there will be hell to pay! Do you understand me?"

"Yes, sir!" was the frightened recruit's reply. Sure enough, when it came time to pee for the test, he couldn't.

The DI was inches from his face. "You had better take your tiny little prick into that head and piss in my cup! And you had better do it right fucking now, recruit. Go piss in my fucking cup!" Everything at MCRD belongs to the drill instructor—even the tiny plastic cups meant to hold urine.

"This recruit can't, sir!"

The DI didn't take his eyes off the recruit standing in front of him. "Classroom, circle!" he shouted at the rest of us. This was the command that told us to gather in a half-circle, facing the drill instructor.

"Everybody turn around!" We were all now facing away from the DI and the recruit who couldn't pee. We could not see what was going on, but we could hear.

"Drink!" The DI handed the recruit a canteen of water. The recruit took the canteen and started drinking. He got about halfway through it and stopped.

"Keep drinking! You will not stop drinking until you can piss in my cup!"

The recruit finished the canteen and was handed

another one. Now the DI had stopped shouting. He simply made demands in a calm, authoritative voice. "Drink." Another canteen was handed to the recruit. "Drink."

The recruit continued to drink until his stomach rebelled against the sheer quantity of fluid and he puked all over the floor.

"What the fuck is this? What the FUCK is this? First, you can't piss in my cup, and now you're puking all over my floor. CLEAN THIS SHIT UP! And you will piss in my cup, recruit! Is that understood? Before this day is over, you WILL piss in my cup!"

A small part of me felt pity for my fellow recruit, but a larger part of me was thinking, *I'm glad it's not me.*

It was at that moment that I realized that there is absolutely *no way* to be "ready" for Marine Corps boot camp. Marine Corps drill instructors are professional assholes. Yelling, insulting, degrading—it's an art form to them. If you have a soft spot they will find it, and poke it over and over again until you either crack or the soft spot becomes hard. They are relentless, and they are proud of it. Their only job is to make Marines. And Marines do not get to have soft spots.

As for the physical part, although I was much better off than many, it was still excruciating. My fitness going in did not matter. They simply exercised me to absolute exhaustion, time and time again. They had ways to make muscles hurt that I didn't know I had.

Top all this with the fact that I was getting an average of four or five hours of sleep a night, and you might begin to understand the hell I was in. There was not a single moment of the day, from reveille to taps, in which I did not want to stop and take a break. Every ounce of my being was begging for a break. A break never came. After two weeks, I wanted to quit so bad that I seriously contemplated telling them I was gay so that I could get out.

There were only two things that made these three months of my life even remotely tolerable—chow time and mail call. Chow is self-explanatory. Short as they were (usually about fifteen or twenty minutes), breakfast, lunch, and dinner were the only consistent breaks throughout the day.

Mail call was a double-edged sword. If I got mail, it was like winning the lottery. This probably has to do with the fact that everybody in boot camp, at one time or another, feels like the most useless piece of shit on the planet. The whole thing is designed to make you feel that way. That doesn't change the reality of the feeling. A care package, or a letter, or a postcard was a reminder that there were people in the world that cared about me. A lack of mail left me feeling empty and dejected.

It was while living in this hellish environment that I received my first-ever letter from Brynn. It was four pages, single-spaced, typed. I know this because I kept it, just as I kept every letter from her; and I still have them today. They were letters from a beautiful girl. To say that they were worth their weight in gold degrades their value considerably. I would only learn many years later that she also kept my letters.

For three months, we wrote back and forth. Every letter from her was an explosion of goodness that washed over me, erasing the hard reality of my existence. I can remember one evening receiving a letter from Brynn while doing the field training portion of boot camp at Camp Pendleton. Our platoon was bivouacked atop one of the many hills of the base. I had just bathed and shaved with a single canteen of ice-cold water, and tried to warm myself as I read her letter and watched the sun set over the Pacific Ocean.

In her letter she wrote that she was in San Clemente at

her grandfather's beach house. San Clemente is maybe ten miles from the place we were camped. I felt a simultaneous thrill and pang of regret at our proximity.

I read the letter two or three times before I was interrupted by the *pop* and flash of a magnesium flare that floated down from the sky. That flare usually meant that someone had left their rifle unsecured and a DI had picked it up. *Oh, shit!*

I had been so caught up in the letters and the beauty of the setting sun that I wasn't certain where my rifle was. I frantically looked around and breathed a sigh of relief when I spotted my rifle, right where it should be. I put away the letter, someplace where I could find it easily so I could read it again the next night, and the night after that.

I wrote her back as frequently as I could manage, stealing time to write on Sundays in chapel or on Fire Watch in the wee hours of the morning. Whenever I could sneak a minute, I would, even if it meant risking getting in serious trouble, because I didn't want the letters to stop. I was deathly afraid the letters would stop.

And so I survived MCRD San Diego by breaking up the impossible day into small survivable chunks of time. After breakfast, I focused on surviving until lunch. After lunch, I focused on making it to dinner. After dinner, I looked forward to mail call where I hoped for a letter from Brynn. It's a technique that served me well fifteen years later when I faced impossible days in an even lower rung of hell.

In the end, MCRD had done its job. I was a different man on graduation day than I was going in. Some changes were the indirect results of the environment. My lips were dry and cracking, my nose was peeling from the sun, and my voice, after three months of screaming, was nothing more than a hoarse whisper. But other results were the direct intention of the program. I was physically stronger and tougher than I ever had been before. I was capable of running three miles in under eighteen minutes, doing 100 sit-ups in two minutes and doing twenty pull-ups. More than that, though, I was mentally tougher. I had the newfound confidence that only comes from experiencing hardship and coming out on the other end.

Photo of the Author Taken upon Graduation from Marine Corps Recruit Depot, San Diego, CA

The sixty-plus Marines of platoon 2012 also made it through that hell with me, and it was as a cohesive unit that we marched around the parade deck on graduation day, our footsteps in perfect unison, chests out, and chins up. We were Marines.

After we had been ordered to "fall out," we congratulated each other. We then quickly made our way to the bleachers where our families and friends all waited. There in the stands, watching the ceremonies, were my mom, dad, sister, and my three roommates and dear friends, Tommy, John, and Josh. Sitting with them, all the way from Los Angeles, was Brynn.

I was ecstatic to see all of them. But I was indescribably happy to see Brynn. I'd almost forgotten how beautiful she was, and I hate to admit it, but what first grabbed my attention was her ass. She wore a pair of slacks that hugged her in all the right places. I was awestruck then and, to this day, I feel it to be one of God's greatest masterpieces. When I realized I was ogling, I quickly raised my eyes to her face, and she smiled. This was the first time I saw the marvelous dimple in her left cheek that only appears when her smile reaches her eyes. It's a dimple that I will go to the ends of the earth using all my charm and humor to make appear as often as I can.

There I was, surrounded by my family and three of my best friends, and this beautiful young thing was there to see me. She gave me a kiss on the cheek and whispered "Congratulations" in my ear. I was flying.

After graduation and introducing everybody to my DIs, we headed out to lunch as a group. My parents and sister went in their car, and I climbed into the back of John's brand-new Jeep. The blue paint shimmered in the sun and the beige interior still had that new-car smell. Brynn sat next to me.

The sun was shining, the top was down, and as we

pulled onto the freeway the wind ripped through the car, blowing Brynn's hair all over the place. John turned up the music in response to the increased wind, and we flew down the freeway. It was a great day.

From there, somebody took me to pick up one of my fellow Marines, Private Apjoke, or "Apjoker," as he was now known to those of us from platoon 2012. His family had been unable to make it out to California for the graduation, and I wasn't going to let him hang out alone in a hotel room on graduation day. There was a party that night that my friends knew about, so I invited him to join us.

The party was your typical college fare. Lots of young men and women crammed into somebody's little apartment, music blaring, and enough alcohol to open a small liquor store. It was fun but quite a contrast to boot camp. After three months of sleep deprivation and having our body clocks trained to rack out at about 8:00 p.m., both Apjoke and I were exhausted before the party even started. At about ten o'clock I asked around to see if somebody could give Apjoke a ride back to the hotel.

"I've been drinking, but you can take my car," Brynn told me. "I'll go with you guys."

I was secretly very pleased.

On the way to the hotel, Apjoke asked if we could stop by a gas station to pick up some snacks for his hotel room. We pulled over, Apjoke went in, and Brynn and I were alone for the first time.

What we talked about, I can't remember. All I can remember is that it was dark in the car. Brynn's face was lit only by the ambient light from the gas station. Despite the darkness, I noticed a hint of mischief in her eyes.

With no more warning than that, she reached across the car, put her arms around me and began to kiss me. My heart now pounding with intense pleasure, I kissed her back. It was a *great* day.

As Apjoke came out of the store and found us making out in the front seat of the car, he gave a loud "Woohoo!," embarrassing the both of us into stopping.

We dropped off Apjoke at the hotel and went back to our house at Rincon St., where we continued our make-out session until everybody else returned home from the party.

It was the single best day of my life, a day in which the universe seemed to align to provide me with the perfect twenty-four hours. I can remember thinking to myself at the time, *How will I ever explain this incredible day to my future wife and leave out the best part—kissing this beautiful girl.*

CHAPTER FIVE
Wednesday

Wednesday, December 2, 2009

The day after Anthony's birth started as such a truly wonderful day. Anthony was doing well. We had already learned that he was off of supplemental oxygen, which was an excellent sign that, despite his size, his lungs were developed.

As if to rejoice in that fact, Mother Nature painted her sky with vibrant white clouds and lit them with an intense sunlight that made me squint behind my sunglasses. I felt energized by the day so I decided to go into work for a few hours to take care of some things. Right around noon, Brynn called me. Her dad, Alan, had come to the hospital and wanted to visit Anthony. One of Anthony's parents needed to accompany him, and she was unable to. She asked if I could come and take Alan to the NICU.

After delivering Anthony, Brynn had been moved up to the fifth floor to the postpartum area of the hospital. I made my way up there, noting that the hospital was in the midst of taking down the Thanksgiving decorations and replacing them with Christmas tinsel and trees and Santa Clauses.

I thought hopefully, *Maybe he'll be home in time for Christmas.*

I found Alan in Brynn's room, visiting with his daughter,

and the two of us went down to the NICU. Unfortunately, at the time we tried to visit, Anthony was in the midst of having an IV inserted.

The NICU nurse stood on the other side of the window and spoke to me on the phone, "When they're so small, it takes some time for us to insert the IVs. Why don't you come back in about twenty minutes."

"I've got to get back to work. I don't think I'll be able to wait that long," Alan told me.

We were both disappointed, but what could be done? I said good-bye to my father-in-law and headed back to the fifth floor to hang out for a bit with my wife. Brynn was lying on her hospital bed, still wearing the hospital gown she so hated.

"Dad didn't get to see him," I told her.

"Why not?" Worry creeping into her voice. Fear had been living with us for so long that we had both picked up the bad habit of assuming the worst.

"Don't worry, there's nothing wrong with Anthony. He was just having an IV inserted."

"Oh, okay. Well, that was shitty timing."

"Yeah. I thought I'd stick around for a while and hang out with my beautiful wife. What do you think?"

"I'd love that," she said with excitement. She knew this was a big offer on my part, as I am profoundly uncomfortable in hospitals. I have a physical reaction nearing panic when I walk into them. I hate them. But I wanted to be with my wife, so I stayed and calmed myself with a game of solitaire on her laptop.

While I was there, Dr. Wigi came into the room.

"Hello, Brynn, How are you feeling today?" His air of confidence had returned in full force, but he also seemed genuinely pleased to see her. He palpated her tummy and checked her sutures. "Everything seems to be healing well. Any pain?"

"A little, but not too bad." Brynn had delivered our

three other children without the benefit of an epidural. The discomfort associated with the C-section was minimal compared to that.

"When do you think I'll be able to go home?" she asked.

"Probably a couple more days, maybe three. But I don't think any longer than that."

"Good. I've got a ton of Christmas shopping to do."

"Okay. I'll be in to check on you again."

When he left, the nurse helped her from the bed so that she could go to the bathroom. I turned from the computer to watch the nurse help her back to the hospital room chair. The nurse left us alone. I went back to my solitaire and just like that, my life changed forever.

I don't know why I turned back to her. I don't know if she was talking and suddenly stopped, or if I sensed something was wrong. Whatever the reason, I turned, and when I did, her head was laying back over the top of the chair.

I was startled but not unduly concerned. I thought she passed out. Brynn had fainted once before only days after giving birth to Grace. I called the nurse. She came in and attempted to wake her with smelling salts. When she did not come to, the nurse slapped my wife across the face. "Come on, Brynn! Just a little too much walking today. Come on, honey, wake up!" When Brynn would still not wake up, the nurse sent me for help.

Dr. Wigi was still on the fifth floor, filling out paperwork, and was able to respond immediately. He came into the room and quickly examined my wife. His demeanor changed instantly. The man that seemed to radiate confidence suddenly had an edge to his voice and concern written on his face. "We need to get her on the bed!"

I helped him and the nurse lift my wife's limp body onto the hospital bed. As we lifted her, I could see that her IV had popped out and the blood from her arm smeared my shirt and shorts.

I stood aside and watched the doctor examine my wife. I can only imagine the vacant look on my face. It was becoming clear that she had not simply passed out. She was having some sort of seizure. Occasionally, she seemed to gasp for air, but she was like a recently caught fish flopping on the shore. No matter how hard she tried, she could not breathe. I left the room so that they could work.

Amazingly, I can actually remember being some-what sedate at this point. My wife could not breathe, but I was calm. I was rationalizing. No, I was denying. *I'm in a hospital. They will fix this fast. Whatever it is, they will fix it.* The "this could never happen to me" part of my psyche was still in control.

My memory, from this point on, is a bit choppy. Information seemed to come at me in random and spo-radic bursts of visual and audio. There is no chronology to my memory. There are only memories that I later had to paste together as well as I could.

Nobody was telling me anything directly. What I learned, I picked up from the conversation around me.

"Call the code," said the doctor.

"This phone doesn't work," was the anonymous re-ply.

"I don't care! Go find one that works and call the code!"

I had no idea at the time what "calling a code" meant. I was only aware of a frantic energy that seemed to build as new people became aware of my wife's condition. It was a palpable sense of panic kept barely contained under the veneer of professionalism. Though nobody wanted to panic, they could not hide their expressions. They could not hide their body language. And some could not keep back the occasional, "Oh my!" or "Oh no!"

The dread built up inside me as the reality of what was happening became clearer. It was only kept in check by my strong sense of denial. It was kept in check until I heard the words, "Begin CPR." Those words sparked a fear so intense, so primal, that it exploded within me, shattering the dam of denial and washing through every part of my being like a polluted river. The river of fear made me sick to my stomach, and I choked back the bile that rose in my throat.

It was a Wednesday. It was supposed to be a day of celebration.

CHAPTER SIX

A Category Five Hurricane

San Jose, California, 1999

The age of twenty is not necessarily the best age to meet the love of your life. I'm sure for some people, it works out fine, but it did not for Brynn and me. There was a weight and an intensity to our relationship... a weight and intensity that we both felt, and neither of us was capable of supporting. We were young and naïve and, basically, neither of us was ready to "settle down." So, after that wonderful day of my graduation from MCRD San Diego, Brynn and I saw each other a couple more times but then went our separate ways.

***

Five years later, in the summer of 1999, I was living back in my hometown of San Jose after having "boomeranged" backed to my parents' home. I took a road trip down to San Diego to visit my SDSU friends. While at Josh's apartment, I saw a picture of Brynn on his wall. He had a collage of all the people who were important to him, and there she was, as beautiful as ever.

"How's Brynn been?" I asked.

I was a bit tentative because I knew how protective Josh was. I guess I didn't have to be. He didn't seem offended by the inquiry at all. "She's fine, I guess. I have her email address if you want it."

"Uh, sure. Maybe I'll drop her a line when I get back," I said, as nonchalant as I could manage.

The first thing I did as soon as I got home to my computer was to send Brynn an email. We began to correspond regularly.

In that time, I found out that she was dating one of her sister's professors from the junior college. Lucky for me, he did not know what he had. Not so lucky for him, Brynn was not complaining about the relationship to one of her girlfriends. She was complaining about it to me—and I had ulterior motives. I became a master of insinuation.

"He never calls me. I always have to call him," she complained to me.

"I don't know, Brynn. Maybe he's just busy. On the other hand, how long does it take to make a phone call?"

At every opportunity I reminded her of how special she was and how she deserved the absolute best when it came to a man. I never said I was that man; I only gently suggested that he was not. And then it happened. He made a fatal mistake and stood her up. I pounced.

"You should come on up to San Jose for a mini-vacation. Just get away from it all for a while. We'll go up to the city"—when you live in San Jose, "the city" means San Francisco—"do all the tourist stuff. It'll be fun."

To my great pleasure she agreed. She talked her friend Janette into going with her, and the plan was for them to come up during the Christmas break.

I was so excited about her coming up that I made a mistake in the directions I gave her, telling her to take the 156 instead of the 152; and they got lost. This was a horrible start. First, I felt like an idiot for giving bad directions, and second, I was in agony. It was like I was a kid waiting for Christmas and I had given Santa Clause bad directions. As it turned out, when she finally did arrive, it was better than Christmas.

The door to the downstairs kitchen was the most often used entrance to the house, and I had told Brynn to come to that door when she arrived. I was standing next to the kitchen island when she walked through the door.

There's something that I need to mention here; Brynn has, since the day I've known her, greeted EVERYBODY with a hug. It is a part of who she is. And I must admit that I love to watch all my big "tough" friends squirm uncomfortably as she pulls them into her embrace. But I love it even more to watch them finally give in and hug back. It is definitely part of her charm.

She hugged me, as she hugs everybody, and I hugged her back. But there was a little more to the hug. She looked me in the eye and said three very simple words. "I missed you."

Like an ocean wave wiping out the walls of a sand castle, three words crushed any barrier that had been between us. "I missed you, too." I said.

After six years, within five minutes of seeing each other, we kissed again.

Chemistry—Brynn and I were like hydrogen and oxygen coming together to produce fire and heat and water. It was an undeniable physical fact of nature that we should be together. We stood there, in my parents' kitchen, holding each other tightly, our hearts pounding against each other, our lips pressed together as though no time or distance had ever been between us. Yes, much better than Christmas.

The visit only got better from there. The next day we went into the city. Janette came with us. It was a remarkably sunny day for San Francisco, though the city's ever-present breeze was made evident by the clouds whipping by over our heads.

"You gotta have some clam chowder. Come on. We'll go down by the water." And we did. I found an open-air fish market that sold clam chowder in a sourdough bowl. The three of us devoured the treat as we sat by the bay.

We did all the other touristy things like taking the cable cars and walking around Union Square. And of course, I took them to the Golden Gate Bridge. There, the wind, unhindered by skyscrapers and hills, whipped into the inlet of the San Francisco Bay.

"I'm cold," Brynn said to me, shivering as we walked.

I gave her my sweatshirt to protect her from the chill and, as we walked across the Golden Gate, we held hands. The touch of her hand, so soft, sent a jolt throughout my body. It could have been snowing and I would have been plenty warm. It just felt so right, walking alongside her, holding her hand.

Brynn and Janette stayed for four days, and in those days, Brynn and I at least came to terms with our physical attraction to each other. It would take months for us to reconcile everything else.

You see, there are more reasons that Brynn and I should *not* be together than there are to explain why we do so well together. If you were to take a logical, systematic approach to our relationship, you would invariably come to the conclusion that we do not belong together. The simple reality is that, "on paper," Brynn and I are a horrible match.

I am an adventurer. I don't say that to try and romanticize myself. It is the simple truth of who I am. I am the guy that enjoys spending two weeks in the Sierras with nothing more than what I can carry on my back. I am the guy that hitchhikes from San Diego to Riverside because I want to see my sister, and I don't have a car. I am the guy who drives down to Rosarito, Mexico, by myself in my beat-up old car, taking dirt back roads because I don't have money for the toll road. I am a kite.

Brynn is not a kite. She is perfectly at ease sitting at home for hours on end, reading books or watching movies. Brynn is the girl who loves her rules. If the sign says "NO RIGHT TURN ON RED," then she will not turn. It does not matter if there is not another car in any direction for miles; Brynn will not turn. She cannot tolerate being late; she will not send her children out into the world unless their hair is combed and their teeth are brushed. Brynn is an anchor.

Beyond our own personal makeup, we are also very different people with regard to politics, religion, and just about every other "important" subject. She is VERY Catholic. I am not even baptized. She is VERY Republican. Let's just say, in 2000, I voted for Ralph Nader. She is a teacher. I was suspended from school six times from elementary school through high school.

These facts had me convinced that Brynn was nothing like the woman I needed to be with. In my twenty-six years of living, I had convinced myself that the women I should be dating were "kites" like me.

I wanted athletic, adventurous women who would want to backpack the Sierras and make trips to Africa, run marathons in Hawaii. I was certain that was what I needed to lead a happy and fulfilling life—*I was certain.*

She, of course, had similar reservations. Tall, dark, handsome, Catholic, and successful were all on her checklist. I'm five-foot-six (a full inch shorter than Brynn). I have a skin tone that's just this side of translucent; I'm definitely not Catholic and I was waiting tables at the time. The closest I come to any of those is "handsome," and all I can say about that is, I'm glad she's got a great deal of tolerance in that category.

There was no denying the attraction, however, and

so we let that be enough for a time. We both told each other we were not ready for a serious relationship and so allowed ourselves the fun of each other's company with no greater expectation.

It was during this non-exclusive period in our young relationship that I actually went in search of the "kite" that I thought I wanted.

My "kite" was a girlfriend that I had met while at San Diego State. She, like me, sought adventure and travel. Where I joined the Marine Corps, she joined the Peace Corps. She was stationed in Mali, which was, at the time, the third-poorest country in the world per capita.

Months prior to Brynn's visit (while Brynn was still dating the professor, mind you), the opportunity arose for me to go and visit this girl in Mali. I was certain that this was *exactly* the kind of girl I thought I needed. I also knew that traveling to Africa was likely to be a once-in-a-lifetime opportunity and I took it.

It took months to plan the trip. I got a passport and a visa from the Malian embassy and chalked up a bunch of credit card debt to purchase my plane tickets. To save money I would be flying out of LAX.

There is no doubt that this was a very perplexing time for me. By the time the trip had arrived, Brynn and I had reconnected. I was torn and confused, and I had no idea what to do. I remember having a discussion about my situation with my good friend, Tommy, who had let me crash at his place before flying out of LAX. I don't remember much of the discussion, but I vividly remember his characterization of Brynn. "She's the kind of girl you marry."

Marriage—not something I had even considered.

Glendora, where Brynn was living at the time, is about thirty miles east of Hollywood, where I was staying at Tommy's. It was too close for me to not drive out to see her before getting on my plane. It was a visit that would simply add to my confusion. There I was, spending a wonderful evening with one girl, but leaving the very next day to go spend three weeks in Africa with another. I know, to many guys this sounds like a great situation. For me it was torture.

To this day, I thank God for that trip. In the three weeks I spent traveling, I learned more about myself and my world and the people in it than I did in four years of college. I learned what it was like to be a minority, as I was often the only white guy for miles around. I learned how frightening and infuriating it can be to not speak the language. I learned that poor people, though living in miserable conditions, can still find joy in family and friendship; and I learned how unbelievably fortunate I was to have been born in the United States. I also learned that when two "kites" come together, they eventually end up tangling their tales.

Three weeks in a third-world country, and it was apparent to all involved that this girl and I were not meant for each other. I'd be lying if I said I wasn't surprised. But there was no denying it. And so I came home from Mali, enlightened. I can't say whether it was on that trip or shortly after that trip, but at some point I had an epiphany. And by epiphany, I mean I finally realized how STUPID I was being. Brynn was a beautiful woman, a wonderful person, and for some unknown reason, she liked me—despite my numerous deficits. Finally, I was able to see her for what she *was* instead of what she *wasn't*.

Brynn has a word for these moments in life. She calls them "God moments." Getting my head out of the way so that I could see how perfect she was for me was definitely a "God moment." And as soon as my head was out of the way, my heart took over. With my heart in control, it would not take long for me to fall head over heels in love with her.

THE HAKONE JAPANESE GARDENS, SARATOGA, CALIFORNIA, 2000

It was early spring, only a few months after my trip to Mali, and Brynn and I held hands as we followed the winding path up the hill into the lush vegetation that surrounded us. We were enjoying the beauty of the Hakone Gardens and enjoying being together.

The Hakone Gardens is a Japanese-style tea garden nestled into the base of the lush green Santa Cruz Mountains. Koi ponds, manicured stone and gravel paths, and beautiful woodwork all enhance the natural beauty of the garden itself. Its entire purpose is tranquility and it achieves its purpose perfectly.

As we walked, we talked about marriage. We spoke bluntly and matter-of-factly about subjects ranging from where we might live to whether we wanted children. Neither of us took the institution lightly. We both took it as the most serious commitment.

For Brynn, there were religious implications; for me, it was an issue of honor. You do not promise to love somebody, for better or for worse, until death, and then go back on your promise. If you can't live up to it, then you don't make the promise.

We both needed to be sure. But there was no way to be sure. Neither of us had an answer. We could not see the future. We could not know how we might feel in five…twenty…fifty years. We were in love, but we knew too much of the world to not have doubt.

Furthermore, we were not the only ones to have any doubt about our relationship. In the previous months, our friends and our families were convinced that we were both nothing short of insane. By most definitions, we probably were. Our homes were 360 miles apart. We were both living with our parents, and we were suddenly dating after a six-year separation. Yes, "madly" in love was more than just an expression with us.

About halfway up the hill, we stopped at a resting place. It was a bench beneath a massive cherry tree. The trees were in full bloom and the canopy surrounded us with a cloud of pinkish-white blossoms. "Is this real?" I asked her.

"I don't know. It feels real. Can we pray about it?"

At that point in my life, though I believed in God, I was not in the habit of praying about things or asking God for signs. I don't think I believed he worked that way. But when the girl you love asks you to do something—well, let's just say, I didn't see the harm in asking.

It was cool in the shade of the tree, so we huddled close together for warmth, held hands, and asked for a sign. More accurately, she asked for a sign. "Dearest Lord, please give us a sign that this is real and this is true."

Another God moment—There we were, holding each other and looking into each other's eyes, searching for answers we did not have. Suddenly, a stiff breeze blew through the garden. It raised the temperature about ten degrees, causing us to shiver, and blew life into the blossoms surrounding us. As they were blown from the tree, they floated on the breeze that swirled about us, a swirling cloud of pink and white, each blossom a voice in a silent chorus. The chorus sang to us in unspoken words—words that Brynn and I knew instantly to be the voice of God, *You two are perfect for each other.*

Decisive (or impulsive) as I am, I did not see any reason to put things off any longer. I figured when God starts blowing cherry blossoms around you, you've probably found *the One.*

In April 2000, I flew down to Glendora and surprised Brynn. She answered the door in her pajamas after a horrible day at work.

Her sister, who had known I was coming, tried to get her to put some clothes on by telling her a friend was stopping by, but Brynn did not heed the warning. As she opened the door, she saw me, down on one knee, holding out roses in my right hand and a diamond ring in my left. She cried and shrieked with delight and surprise. It was a wonderful moment for me to see how happy I made her with my humble request to be my bride. It was April 26, 2000. Only a short four months after our Christmas break reunion.

Yes, our romance was not a whirlwind. It was a straight up, category five hurricane.

GLENDORA, CALIFORNIA, 2000

About five minutes after I proposed to Brynn, she began to plan our wedding. They proceeded as do the plans of many. We struggled to balance unrealistic expectations with the realities of our financial situation. We lucked into our reception site when I (the kite) picked up and dragged Brynn (the anchor) through the doors of a restaurant that was not even open and was still under construction at the time.

"We can't go in there," Brynn protested.

"Sure we can. Look, the door's open."

"Yeah, for the construction workers!"

"Come on; let's go see."

We ended up meeting Manuél, the owner of the restaurant, and because we were the first party he had ever booked, he gave us a ferocious bargain—We would pay only twenty-five dollars a plate *and* he sold us all of our wine at cost. This was a tremendous coup for us.

And that was kind of how our wedding planning went. It wasn't as if it was not work, but time and again we lucked into chance meetings that went our way. We found our florist when Brynn and I were attending the wedding of one of Brynn's friends. Brynn commented on how beautiful the centerpieces were, and a lady sitting at the table with us (a total stranger at the time) said, "Well, thank you. I put these together." Her name was Sherri and, not only did she end up being our florist, she was the florist for every friend of ours we could convince to use her.

Detail after detail would come together for the big day—all except for one minor detail. We could not find a priest. For many Catholics, this might not seem all that irregular. There are only a limited number of priests out there, and it is sometimes hard to find one for big events. For Brynn's family, however, this was quite shocking. They are close personal friends with about half of the archdiocese of Los Angeles (this is only a slight exaggeration). Yet everyone they asked was unable to do it.

The first priest Brynn asked was her dear friend, Monsignor Pierce. He was a fiery and cantankerous old Irishman who had been the pastor of the church Brynn went to as a child, St. Louise De Marillac. He had watched Brynn grow up, and had even been her boss when she had worked in the church office as a young lady. Unfortunately, Monsignor Pierce was getting on in age, and his health was not so great. He worried that he would not feel well enough when the day finally came.

Our next option was Father Brian, the pastor at Sacred Heart Church where Brynn's mom worked as a secretary. Unfortunately, Father Brian was going to be in Ireland for the date we had set.

Father Chris, then the current pastor of St. Louise, was also going to be on vacation. So, we asked Father Martin, a young Nigerian priest and very close friend of ours who I played soccer with on Sundays. Father Martin, though incredibly sweet, is also incredibly shy and soft-spoken. He simply refused, telling us he was willing to be the co-celebrant but that he would be too nervous to be the celebrant on such a special occasion.

When they had exhausted all of their local possibilities,

they decided to take a long shot on a priest who had once been an associate pastor at St. Louise. This priest, Father Tim, had moved up north to Petaluma (about 430 miles to the north) where he was teaching. He was a close friend of the family, but they knew it would be a great deal to ask of him to fly down here for a single wedding. Much to everybody's delight, he said yes. It would turn out to be a very fortuitous turn of events, because Father Tim was exactly the kind of priest we would need for this very unique wedding.

JULY 14, 2001 COVINA, CALIFORNIA

I arrived at the church after having spent the previous night in a local hotel with my family and some of the groomsmen. When I got there I was let into the sacristy where I met with Father Tim. I sat back there talking with him when, much to our surprise, an older gentleman came shuffling down the hall. He was gripping onto his cane, moving as though every step was painful. He was wearing black pants, a black shirt, and a priest's collar. It was Monsignor Pierce, Brynn's cantankerous, old, former boss.

Monsignor Pierce, though he suffered great pain and discomfort due to his health, decided he did not want to miss our ceremony. Father Tim quickly hid the look of surprise on his face and welcomed the older priest. They went about discussing who would do what during the wedding, when in walked Father Martin. Though he had said he would co-celebrate, we hadn't heard anything from him in the weeks before the wedding and so thought Father Tim would be flying solo—Nope.

Where we were once unable to find a priest, we now had three all gearing up to marry us. Then Father Brian walked in. He had decided to postpone his vacation because he, also, did not want to miss the wedding. The sacristy was now packed with priests. We would also find out later that one of Father Martin's friends, another priest from Africa, had come to watch the wedding from the pews because he had never seen an American wedding before.

The ceremony went off without a hitch. Father Tim took the time to explain everything that was being done to educate the non-Catholics in the crowd—mostly my side of the church. He was humorous and entertaining and brought a lightness to the ritual that was appreciated by all. Then, he gave the floor to Monsignor Pierce.

Now, I had met Monsignor before and I knew he thought highly of Brynn. But he would show his respect for her in a very strange way. Every time we met, he would joke with me, "Are you sure you know what you're getting into? It's not too late to back out. She's a handful. Nobody will think less of you."

The funny thing is he actually reminded me of myself. To this day, the way I am most comfortable showing affection is by making fun of people. I don't make fun of people I don't like. I don't even waste my breath on them. It is the people I love that I poke fun at. Monsignor was the exact same way. And as much as he made fun of Brynn, it was obvious to me that he loved her very much.

To show his love, he came to our wedding, despite being wracked with arthritis and suffering any number of other ailments. Not only did he come to our wedding, he had also gone to extraordinary lengths to get Brynn and me an apostolic blessing from Pope John Paul II.

An apostolic blessing is a certificate that has been blessed by the pope himself, and is a pretty big deal among Catholics. It was to be his big finale to present this very special blessing to us at our wedding.

Unknown to Monsignor until that day, however, Brynn and I had already been given an apostolic blessing from another priest friend of theirs who worked at the Vatican

(I told you they were VERY Catholic). As he presented our *second* apostolic blessing, he would again show his love for Brynn by teasing her.

He stood on the altar in front of the some 250 people who had gathered to celebrate our nuptials, but when he spoke, he spoke directly to us. He referred to the multiplicity of priests at the wedding and then to the *two* apostolic blessings we received, and set himself up for the perfect punchline. "Perhaps the Lord was trying to tell us something..." He paused for dramatic effect. "Kyle—you're going to need all the blessings you can get."

The entire church erupted in laughter.

On our wedding day, it was the sweet humor of a loving old man. He couldn't know that nine years later he would be absolutely right.

Monsignor Robert Pierce Delivering
Brynn and Kyle's Second Apostolic Blessing

The Newlyweds

CHAPTER SEVEN
Blue

Cyanosis: a blue coloration of the skin and mucous membranes due to the presence of large amounts of deoxygenated hemoglobin in blood vessels near the skin surface.

Anaheim Regional Medical Center, December 2, 2009, sometime around 2:30 p.m.

"Code Blue, Tower Five East ... Code Blue, Tower Five East."

Code Blue is the hospital terminology for a patient in cardiac arrest. It is also the color of a person who is not getting oxygen into their system. Brynn was now turning blue.

I was in the hallway outside my wife's room. I was in my stocking feet with her blood on my shirt and shorts. She was dying only twenty feet away from me. I could do nothing.

In seconds, I was surrounded. Her room, already filled to capacity, was now boiling over with people in scrubs—doctors, nurses, I couldn't tell you. There must have been thirty people there. Yet I was as alone as I have ever been. Time was doing that strange thing that it does in crisis, slowing down, turning over on itself so that the memories are a jumbled puzzle. The staccato bursts of information were filling my ears and my eyes.

"I can't find a pulse."

"There's a weak pulse."

"She's breathing. If she's breathing, she has a pulse."

Mixed in with the chaos was a vision of my future. It only lasted two or three seconds before I could shove it out of my mind, but that was long enough. It was a future without my wife, a vision of me as a single father of four, and I was failing at it. The vision terrified me.

"We've talked about this!" I began shouting at God there in the hallway. "We've had this discussion! I can't do this without her! You know this! I CAN'T DO THIS WITHOUT HER!" I was furious with him and I did not hold back my anger.

Somebody came up to me. "Would you like me to get you a chair? You should sit down."

"I couldn't possibly sit down!" I muttered. I knew they were simply trying to be kind. My mind was beginning to realize that I was the center of a tragedy and people were going to want to help. But the thought of sitting seemed insane to me. My heart was thudding inside my chest as my adrenal glands flooded my bloodstream with their product. I had to move. I had to run. I had to run until exhaustion overcame the fear. But their eyes were all on me. Suddenly I was in the spotlight of the world. I was at the center of a tragic event, and the spotlight anchored me to the spot. But I could not stop moving. And so I paced to and fro like a tiger stuck in a cage, all pent-up energy and force. I was at the center and there was no escaping it. My mind spun around the idea…

Center—This isn't happening to me—I am at the center—the center is tragedy and the world is collapsing in on me. This isn't happening to me—their eyes—their faces—filled with pity and sadness. They pity me. They are sad for me. This isn't happening to me. I am tragic and my tragedy is a black hole. It is crushing me. And they feel for me because I am being crushed. They do not know my pain, but they can imagine it—the crushing pain. And the thought hurts them. They hurt for me. This isn't happening to me. They hurt for me and they wish to comfort me. But there is no comfort for this black hole. There is no comfort for this crushing. It is a force of nature, and for now I must endure it alone. I must be crushed. For once I am at the center. And I would give anything to be on the periphery.

Inside the room the techs, nurses, and doctors were valiantly trying to stabilize my wife. They were pumping her heart, administering atropine, doing all they could to get her body to a point that they could move her.

I was standing in the hallway, powerless—absolutely helpless—impotent. There was only one thing I *could* do while I paced up and down the hallway. So I prayed. *Please, God, let them be amazing. Let them be amazing. Let them do their finest work. Let them be amazing.* It became my mantra and I mumbled it to myself and my God as I walked up and down the hallway. *Let them shine. Let them be amazing.*

I can't tell you why this was my prayer. I can't tell you why I didn't pray for something straightforward like, *Please, God, let my wife be okay,* or *Please, God, let her live.* It just struck me that I should pray for the people trying to save her.

Perhaps it is because, since the beginning of my belief in God, I've believed that he does his work through us. We look for him in the supernatural, but most of the incredible work he does is done in the blood, sweat, and tears of his creations. Perhaps my mind thought all of this through. I couldn't say. Even as I prayed, my faith was stretched like an overblown balloon as I tried to believe that he could make this work out. My logical mind worked against hope.

People need oxygen, or they die, or their brains die. People die all the time. FAITHFUL GOOD PEOPLE DIE ALL THE TIME. People who have prayed, just like I was praying, lose people they love ALL THE TIME.

Yet, despite my doubt, I prayed because it was all that I could do. "Please, God, let them be amazing."

"She'll be fine. Everything will be fine." Again somebody was at my shoulder, offering well-meant but perfectly useless platitudes.

I was in no mood to be patronized. "She's purple! Look at her! She's purple!" There was no arguing. Brynn's cyanosis had reached extremes and her skin tone matched that of a hanged man. The platitudes ceased. The chaos did not.

"Where's the ER doctor?"

"Coming from the first floor"

"The elevators aren't working."

"I ran up here from the first! They should be here!"

"Where's your crash cart?"

It seemed an eternity before the ER doctor finally arrived, though it was probably only a few minutes. I was strangely comforted by the fact that it was a woman. Perhaps there was a part of me that hoped she would go a little further or do a little more to help a mother. She took control immediately. "Whoa, what's going on in here? All nonessential personnel get out."

Doctor Wigi, who had initially called the code, gave control to the ER doctor and came out to speak to me.

"We are fairly certain that your wife has had a pulmonary embolism."

Pulmonary—that's lungs. Embolism—I don't know what that is. I should know this! What's that mean?

He seemed to read my confusion and answered the question I couldn't find the words for. "A blood clot, most likely from one of her legs, which had probably formed during her bedrest has broken free and is likely stuck in her pulmonary artery."

Artery—blood—a blocked artery.

"Normally we would give blood thinners to break up the clot. But because she has just had surgery she would bleed too much. They are trying to stabilize her so they can move her to CT, so that we can see the clot and then surgically remove it."

It wasn't until much later that I learned it was a *massive* pulmonary embolism. There were multiple clots occluding the main pulmonary arteries from both the left and right lung. This is the description of the clot from the pathologist.

> The specimen is received in formalin, labeled *Brynn Ervin—blood clot from right and left pulmonary arteries.* It consists of multiple cylindrical portions of rubbery, dark-red thrombus in aggregate weighing 16 grams. These range in length from 0.8 to 10 cm and vary in diameter from 0.1 to 1.7 cm. No other tissue is identified. Representative sections are wrapped and submitted in one cassette.

Sixteen grams of clotted blood stopped my wife's heart. Sixteen grams is a little over half an ounce.

After learning the situation, I knew I would have to make phone calls. I would have to call Alan and Holly (Brynn's parents) and Katie (Brynn's younger sister) and tell them that their Brynn was in serious trouble, and try to hide from them that she might die before they could get to her. I failed in hiding it. Fear was too close to the surface. My entire body rebelled against my mind, and my tongue became lead in my mouth. My words tripped over my leaden tongue as I tried to speak. "Holly," I choked back volumes of saliva, snot, and phlegm, "some... something's wrong with your daughter. They think... they think she's had a pulmonary embolism." My voice was so hoarse and rattled with phlegm from crying that Holly did not recognize me at first.

"Who is this?"

"Your son. You shouldn't drive yourself."

"I'll be right there."

Alan was easier for me, as he did not pick up the phone. The coward in me rejoiced that I only had to leave a message for him. I also called my own parents, who were in town, helping us to prepare for Anthony's arrival. It was getting harder and harder to talk, and so I spoke abruptly. "Brynn's had a pulmonary embolism. It's not good. I need you to get the kids and bring them to the hospital as soon as you can." That was it. That was all I could say.

Some might wonder at my desire to have the kids there during this extreme crisis with their mother. I knew, however, that there would be no keeping this horror from them. They would learn of it anyway, and I felt they needed to be a part of everything. It would be one of the wisest things I've ever done, as it would be those three who brought all the strength and light I needed in the darkest hours.

Not long after I made those phone calls, Brynn was on a gurney and there was somebody straddling her, pumping on her chest. They were moving her so I thought they had stabilized her, but they never did. Her heart was still not beating. They decided to move her anyway. *Please, God, let them do their finest work.*

Her skin was still a deep blue, bordering on purple, from her chest all the way up—textbook indication of a PE. They wheeled her to an elevator. I cannot remember if I took an elevator or the stairs, but I soon found myself down on the first floor being guided to radiology.

By this time, the clot had been lodged in her lungs for thirty minutes or more. Hence, Brynn's brain had been without oxygenated blood for that long. Normally they would "call it." Nobody did. *Let them be amazing.*

Members of the code team traded off, pumping on her chest until they became exhausted.

One courageous tech, still in training at the time, continued to perform chest compressions throughout the ordeal. When the doctor suggested that it was time to "call it," he looked up to the lead nurse with a question in his eyes, "Should I stop?" The answer in her eyes, "It hasn't been long enough." *Let them shine.*

Doctor Wu, Brynn's anesthesiologist from her C-section, also responded to the code. Anticipating the need for an IV for surgery, he, without hesitation, inserted a central line. *Let them do their finest work.*

My parents were the first to arrive with the kids. I saw my dad first and, when I did, I broke down in his arms. "It's bad, Dad. It's real bad." I sobbed into his shoulder. "She's been without oxygen for a real long time. It's so bad." He held me tight in a way he had not had to since I was a small child.

It was my dad that gave me the first thing resembling hope. In his ever-present logic he told me, "They would not be taking her to surgery if there was no hope."

That made sense to me. I knew it was a "snowball's chance" of hope, but there was *some* hope.

Someone from the hospital staff took us to a door. The plaque outside the door read "The Safe Place." I had passed this room many times on my way up to see Brynn while she was on bedrest, and I had always been curious about it. The door had one of those keypad combination locks on it. I had always thought it might be a resting place for tired staff. I soon found that it was a room designed to hide distressed and grieving family members. There were some couches, a television, children's books, and a restroom.

It was in The Safe Place that I saw my children for the

first time. Grace, Isaiah, and Noah came into the room with my mother and Teresa, their nanny.

By this point, my eyes were swollen and red. My children had seen their daddy cry one other time. That was the day I took my dog Trouble to the vet to have her put down. Tears from Daddy were forever linked with death in their minds, and as soon as they saw me, weeping openly, they knew something was wrong. They all moved to comfort me. I hugged them all, and took in a deep breath. It was time to tell my children that their mother might die.

I did not search for the right words, nor did I mince them. The words sat like poison in my mouth, and I wanted to spit them out as quickly as I could. But I needed for them to understand so I spoke slowly and deliberately. "Momma is very sick. The doctors are doing all they can for her right now, but mommy might die." I did not feel safe. Not even remotely.

The words seemed to sink into their minds slowly as though they were sinking into quicksand. Grace was the first to take them in all the way. And as soon as she did, she did the family math. "I can't be the only girl!" she cried.

To us adults, it seemed a strange thing to say, but as I look back on it I think I understand it. She was truly upset at the prospect that her mother, her only companion in the ways of girlhood, might not be there for her tomorrow. In her seven-year-old mind, her mother would be leaving her alone as the only girl in a house full of boys.

As Gracie broke down, her two younger brothers understood this was something that was okay to cry about, and they both broke down as well. They, all three, collapsed in my arms. We hugged so deeply and so tightly, and cried so many tears, you could fill cups with them. But the feeling of my children holding me tight would carry me through the next few hours until they would need to hug me again.

When the hugs were done, Isaiah retreated into himself, as he often does, and made himself busy with a coloring book. Noah, pretty much oblivious to everything, fought with his older brother over the coloring book. The spat was annoying and comforting at the same time. It was a reminder of the normal—a reminder that there was a world out there unconcerned with my tragedy. It was a temporary respite. As new faces entered the room, I saw the truth of my new reality in their hopeless eyes.

Yes, this is happening. I can see it in their faces. My own mind might not comprehend it, but their faces tell the truth of it. It is happening. For the first time in my life, the world is revolving around me; for once all eyes are on me—sunken eyes—crying eyes. I am a celebrity because my wife is dying. I am the train wreck they cannot look away from. Yes, this is happening. I am naked in my fear and in my grief, and they stare at my pain. And so I hug those who love me. I hug them and I hold them tight for long periods of time because they cover me. In hugging them I feel less naked. This is happening and I am mad. I am mad at God because this was not supposed to happen to her.

Away from us, on the CT scan table, Brynn was now no longer blue from the midline up. She was black.

CHAPTER EIGHT

Christmas with the Ervins

Sometime in November 2003, for some unknown reason, I felt compelled to write a Christmas letter, letting all of our family and friends know how our year had gone. As a rule, I do not like family Christmas letters. They tend to be inexpertly veiled, bragging accounts of all the "amazing achievements" of a family. Rarely do they come close to a true reckoning of a family's experience throughout the year.

I did not want to write a letter like that. I wanted to write something that was interesting and fun while at the same time gave all of our friends and family a good understanding of how our year truly went. With this in mind, I sat down at my computer and tried to write something to fulfill all these requirements.

I sat there for two hours staring at a blank screen, perfectly incapable of writing anything. Unable to come up with word one, I went to the kitchen cabinet and pulled out the gin. I mixed a hefty serving with some tonic and some ice from the fridge, cut a wedge of lime, sniffing the citrus smell as I squirted the juice into the cup, plopped the leftover lime wedge into the glass, and got busy relieving myself of my creative inhibitions.

What followed was the very first Ervin family Christmas letter. Reading it now, I can tell I was good and buzzed when I wrote it, but man, was it a fun letter to write. And that letter set the tone for what has become a yearly tradition of me, irreverently and, I hope, humorously letting people know how our lives are going.

Since that first letter I have faithfully sent out a letter every year. There is no better way to know and understand the Ervin family than to read these letters. This is who we are—for better and for worse.

Christmas Letter, 2003

Dear Friends, Family, and those with whom we are marginally acquainted,

Season's greetings and congratulations on being chosen to receive a form letter from the Ervin Clan. "Private Pile, 0311, you made it!"

If you haven't seen *Full Metal Jacket*, then you probably don't get that joke. But it's not my fault you're cinematically illiterate. I blame books!!! They're all over the place! In grocery stores! Online! It's that Harry Potter, I tell you! Oh...uh, Okay, enough of that.

Moving right along, I guess protocol would dictate that I fill you in on all the highlights of our soon dead year. So here goes it.

We Got Disneyland Season Passes!!! The really good ones that get us into the park whenever we want to.

Yep, that's pretty much it. But they're sooooo cool.

Okay, now for the fatherly pride. I've got the most wonderful, splendiferous, and brightest little one-year-old girl in the whole world! Here is but a sampling of her already monstrous vocabulary (listed in order of frequency and importance)

No
Mommy
No Mommy
Poo poo
Pee
Mike (Mike Wizowski from *Monster's Inc.*)
I want Mike
I'm cold. (she really means wet)
No
Dog
Dog No
Baby
No baby
No Dada No (Whenever I try to do anything)
Shoe
Sock
Melmo (Elmo from *Sesame Street*)
I want Melmo.
Dada

Yeah, "Dada" is last on the list, but I've been working on improving my standing with a steady flow of bribes.

Okay, now for husbandly pride. (Side note: Spellcheck is telling me that *husbandly* is not a word. It allows husbandry. But that really isn't what I'm trying to say is it. It also allows fatherly. Why not husbandly? I'm sensing anti-husband-ism. WHAT!!! HUSBSANDISM ISN'T A WORD!!!? Curse those squiggly red lines.)

Anyway, let's get back to what I was saying. To put it lightly, my wife is the eighth wonder of the modern world. First, she deals with a room of 30+ fifth graders all day long, trying to help them navigate the treacherous waters of the California Educational System. Then, she's gotta come home and deal with me and my eccentricities (euphemisms are wonderful aren't they?).

His Holiness John Paul II called me the other day and wants to put her on the super fast track to canonization. I asked, "Doesn't she have to be dead first?" He replied that the fact that she wasn't dead already was one of her miracles. *Don't ever argue with a pope,* is what I always say.

Truly though, she still amazes me on a daily basis with her generous and giving heart and her ability to keep herself above all the craziness. Two years plus into it, and I'm still the luckiest guy on the planet.

Trouble Dog, our Chow-golden retriever mutt, however, is a different story. First off, she has developed an unnatural craving for fully loaded diapers. You can imagine some of the messes that has created!

Furthermore, she has distinguished herself in our neighborhood over the past year by making not one, not two, not even three, but no less than FOUR attempts on the mail lady's life. Sure they'll deliver through rain and sleet, and what have you, but one little puppy gets in the way and it's *wah, wah, wah.*

Hence, if you get a change of address letter soon, telling you that we're now at a P.O. Box, you will know why there is a Chow-golden retriever pelt on eBay for super cheap.

As for me, there is nothing much to brag about. I've been working hard to get my business started (not quite there yet but give me another year.) And I cleaned out the garage. Beyond that I've just been enjoying the heck out of my little girl. Who wouldn't?

We love you all immensely (even those of you with whom we are marginally acquainted), and wish you the greatest fortune in the coming year.

Kyle, Brynn, Gracie, and Trouble Dog

CHAPTER NINE
Moving Oceans

Anaheim Regional Medical Center, December 2, 2009, approximately 3:30 p.m.

All they had to do was stop. Brynn was already "clinically dead" (the medical term for cessation of blood circulation and breathing) and had been for some time. She had been in cardiopulmonary arrest for close to sixty minutes. Her face was now closer to black than blue, or purple. Beyond the embolism, her heart was also in a condition called PEA (pulseless electrical activity). The electrical part of her heart was working but, due to the embolism, the mechanical part of the pump had failed.

All they had to do was stop, and "clinical death" would have almost instantly become "legal death." I would be a widower, and my children would grow up without their mother. All they had to do was stop and there is not a person on the planet, not even me, who could have blamed them. But they did not stop. *Please, God, let them be amazing.*

For over an hour, the men and women of the code team pumped on Brynn's chest—all throughout the CT. One doctor stayed in the CT scanning room, unprotected from the x-rays so that he could pump her chest between scans. They slammed her chest with every ounce of force they could muster, pushing their bodies to physical exhaustion, trying with all their might to get oxygenated blood to her dying cells. *Please, God, let them do their finest work.*

And they did do their finest work. The code team that responded worked with feverish intensity to keep my wife on this side of the knife's edge of death.

When God moves oceans, he can choose to do it all at one time, as he does with the sea currents. Or he can do it one raindrop at a time. To make our miracle, he moved the ocean one raindrop at a time.

One raindrop at a time—the cardiac surgeon is on hand at the hospital and views Brynn's CT scans within minutes of them being developed. He had been on his way to another hospital for another surgery, but that patient had expired.

Brynn, however, was in a very dire state, as is noted in his consultation notes...

Surgeon's Notes (Truncated by the author):

REASON FOR EMERGENCY CARDIOVASCULAR CONSULTATION:
Evaluation of patient with cardiopulmonary arrest and pulmonary emboli undergoing cardiopulmonary resuscitation.

HISTORY OF PRESENT ILLNESS:
This patient is a 34-year-old woman. This patient delivered by cesarean section 24 hours ago. This patient today collapsed in her room. CPR was begun. The patient was found to be blue. The patient was diagnosed as having a pulmonary embolus. She was brought to CT scan, showed still receiving CPR. The patient's diagnosis was confirmed showing emboli in the main pulmonary artery bilaterally. The patient continued to

have CPR and is being brought to the operating room on an emergency basis.

DISCUSSION, RECOMMENDATIONS AND SURGICAL PLAN:
This patient is a candidate for an emergency pulmonary embolectomy. The risks are extremely high for this patient and we have told the family that even if we are successful with the surgery, we do not know of the outcome of her neurological status as she has been receiving CPR for some time. Nonetheless, we will proceed with the surgery as expeditiously as possible.

***

One raindrop at a time—this cardiac surgeon just happens to be one of the very few who knows how to do an emergency pulmonary embolectomy. This procedure has fallen out of favor amongst cardiologists due to its extremely low rate of success. But the surgeon is old enough to have done it before.

The surgeon was there, he knew what to do, but I later learned that he almost decided not to do the surgery. Due to the fact that they had never been able to get Brynn's heart beating again, he feared he could be accused of performing surgery on a dead person. His entire career could be destroyed by this one act. Yet somehow, someway, he found the extreme courage necessary to go forward. *Please, God, let them do their finest work.*

The surgeon is not the only one necessary for such an operation, however. This extremely difficult surgery required an entire team of people.

First, the OR anesthesiologist needed to sedate her and provide all medications necessary to the surgery. To do so he needed to insert a "central line" or CVC (central venous catheter). Fortunately, Brynn already had the central line inserted by Dr. Wu—another raindrop.

Second, the perfusionist is the technician who runs the heart and lung bypass machine—and yet another drop—the hospital's entire team of perfusionists was in the hospital for a training event.

Everybody who needed to be there to save Brynn's life, or more accurately, bring her back from death, was there. Drop after drop, and the ocean was moving. They had Brynn on the operating room table within an hour of when the clot first struck.

***

Our group, now swelling with friends and family who had rushed to the hospital, moved from The Safe Place to the larger surgery waiting room. It was a room directly adjacent to the OR where there were chairs and a couple of loveseats, a television, and a coffee maker.

When we entered the room, the television was on, but after several minutes I realized I was unable to tolerate the additional stimuli. I walked over and turned it off. Our group would suffer in silence. And suffer we did. We had no control over anything. A giant wave had crashed upon us, its sheer mass and momentum sending us twirling and tumbling. We did not know which way was up. We tried to fight against it. We tried to pray it away, worry it away, wish it away. We could not fight against it. It was too massive. We were drowning.

The children, however, showing the wisdom of their youth, and not suffering under the delusion of control, made the best of the situation. In the way children seem to be able to, they relaxed and let the wave take them where it would. There were moments that they cried and were sad. But only minutes later, they converted the waiting room into their own personal playground. Before long they were playing hide-and-seek, crawling under the seats, and chasing each other around the room. I thought about reining them in, but I couldn't do it. Their play made me smile. And so, I decided to join them. Together, we passed the time, climbing under the seats and hiding in the cave-like space under the chairs.

I crawled under one of the seats with Noah, my two-year-old. We curled up together on the dark-green industrial carpet, and I held him as we hid. He held his finger to his lips and said, "Shhhhh." But he said it so loudly everyone in the room could hear. I shushed him back, my face full of mock fear that we might get caught. He smiled. I smiled back. It felt good to hide. It felt good to hold my son in that tight little space. It felt good to be silly. It felt good to play. It felt good to not think about the fact that, only feet away, in the operating room, the surgeon was preparing to slice into my wife's chest.

Christmas Letter 2004

Hello Y'all. 'Tis the season once again! 'Tis the time of fake snow, (well at least here in California) and fake Santas, and real credit card debt. Yep that's right — It's Christmas! And once again you find yourself a member of a privileged few to receive the Ervin Family Christmas letter. Sure it's a form letter that we don't even sign personally but we promise to keep the prints to a minimum so that you can feel appropriately important. Here we go...

Brynn

Brynn, of course, has done it once again. She carried one of my babies in her belly for 10 months forgoing all sorts of worldly pleasures, including but not limited to caffeine, alcohol, and most importantly Dr. Pepper. Then she gave birth to my baby boy... once again without any drugs at all! (Granted she was on a pretty steady flow of Percocet the day after... But who wouldn't be?) Anyway, She went through all that, and she is still as beautiful as the day I met her. Tell me I'm not blessed.

Isaiah

As for baby Isaiah — He was in quite a rush to get into this world. Here's the breakdown:

9:00 PM, November 17 – I instructed my wife that she could not go into labor that night because I was exhausted after a very long day at work. She assured me that she would not because she'd just been to her ObGyn and he told her she's not ready yet. I was comforted because he is a professional.

9:15 PM – I lied down on my couch to watch nothing in particular on TV.

9:30 PM – I was jolted from my dazed state by Auntie Katie telling me something about a broken glass of water. I jumped from the couch, upset with Grace because I was sure she'd been jumping on the bed and knocked over Brynn's water glass. I went to the kitchen and got a trash bag and some kitchen towels.

About half way to the kitchen I realized that Katie had not actually said anything about a glass. What she actually said was, "Kyle, Brynn's water broke!"

9:32 PM – We used every single towel in the house to soak up amniotic fluid.

10:05 PM – I told myself, all right, here we go.

You've done this before. Just keep a cool head.

10:30 PM – While on the way to the hospital that I've been to about 163 times, I made a wrong turn.

10:45 PM – Nana (Holly) beat us to the hospital even though she'd come all the way from Glendora (about 20 miles away).

11:00 PM – The nurse told us we should send everybody home (Brynn's dad had arrived by then) because we had anywhere from 12 to 24 hours until the show started. We were comforted by the nurse's surety because she is a professional.

11:15 PM – Everybody but Brynn and I went home for a good night's sleep.

2:00 AM – November 18 – Another nurse came in and told us that they were going to start a Petosin drip at 6:00 AM if active labor had not started by then. Brynn and I were terrified because we knew that there was no way Brynn could deliver naturally with Petosin induced contractions. Brynn prayed.

3:00 AM – There was no doubt we were in active labor (I say we because it makes me sound more important).

4:00 AM – After one hour of me butchering the 'Our Father' prayer repeatedly, Brynn asked me to call her mom. I thought to myself we're only an hour into this so let's try and let mom sleep for another hour. I told Brynn I'd call her mom at 5:00 AM.

5:00 AM – We had been going through 2 hours of extremely intense labor (and when I say extremely intense I mean that for the first time in my life I was physically afraid of the creature my wife had become).

However, I knew that we had at least 3 or 4 more hours to go. I called Holly, and let her know I could use some relief. Thinking we had plenty of time, I tried to sound as nonchalant as possible.

5:10 AM – We moved from the hospital bed to the bathroom seeking a more comfortable laboring position. I got down on my knees on the bathroom floor and supported Brynn's weight while she endured some incredible contractions. My knees were in agony but I figured complaining about my aching knees to a woman in labor would be a poor idea.

5:30 AM – Brynn's contractions were right on top of each other. She was ready to give up. I told myself these are all the signs of being in transition but it can't be because it was all way too soon.

I lied to my wife and told her that we were almost there.

5:45 AM – Holly arrived to relieve me. My knees were numb and I was gripping on to the plumbing of the toilet with all my might trying to keep Brynn upright. Holly said a few 'Hail Marys' and a couple 'Our Fathers'.

5:50 AM – Brynn said "I have to push!"

I almost shat myself right then and there (Sorry for the vulgarity but sometimes the truth is just ugly). I thought Oh crap! My babies going to be born on the toilet!

Holly ran into the hallway looking for a nurse but could not find anybody. About 30 seconds later I finally got the bright idea to pull the nurse chord that was hanging two feet away on the bathroom wall.

5:52 AM – I was comforted by the fact that, when the nurses came in and found that Brynn was ready to have that baby, they too almost shat themselves right then and there — After all they were the professionals!

5:55 AM – The nurses and I all tried to convince Brynn not to push hard. We wanted the doctor to be there.

Holly had the presence of mind to say, "Oh go ahead and push honey. It's like trying to stop a train." About two contractions later we had a head poppin' out. We weren't going to have a doctor for this one.

6:00 AM – Unfortunately, just like his big sister, Isaiah had gotten the chord wrapped around his neck. It was the only news that could get Brynn not to push. It was then that the nurses shined. They did a wonderful job of getting him untangled and out into the world.

6:06 AM – I'm terrified because little Isaiah came into the world extremely purple and his little body was limp. Not only did he have the chord wrapped around his neck but he had managed to wrap it a couple of times around his body as well. But the nurses quickly got him some oxygen and got him to cry and he pinked up instantaneously.

The rest, as they say, is history.

And as luck would have it, Isaiah was born at a perfect time for this letter to serve as his birth announcement. Not only has he saved me money on paper but on postage as well. He's off to a good start with his old man.

Here's the important info.

Stats:
Born on 11/18/04 at 6:06 AM
Weight – 7 pounds 6 ounces

Lenth – 21 inches (Mom, it looks like he may have gotten the tall gene! Or at least he didn't get the short one.)

APGAR Score – 8 to 9 (This is a bit of information that is totally useless to most of us but my wife seems to be telling everybody so I'm just following suit).

And that's really all you need to know, because other than that he just sleeps, eats, poops and cries. Though, it should be stated that he has already baptized the dining room table. Dinner anyone?

Grace

Grace, so far, has welcomed her baby with open arms. In fact, if she has a fault, it's that she's a bit overaggressive in her affection. One thing's for sure — he's gonna grow up tough.

So far her favorite statements regarding her brother have been:

"He's so tiny. He's so tiny momma!"

"Oh, Isaiah Alan Ervin you're OK." Whenever he cries.

"Hee hee, he pooped. Isaiah pooped daddy."

Speaking of poop, lucky for us, Grace is almost all the way potty trained.

Now that was interesting! I will tell you this — the single greatest benefit to having had dogs all my life is that cleaning poop off the floor is not such a big deal anymore. Yep, she had her moments when she just didn't make it in time. And yeah, I always seemed to get potty duty on such occasions.

Younger gentlemen, and older dudes who think you still might have kids, here is a profound truth of life that you should all take to heart: One of the great disadvantages to having a pregnant wife is that virtually all unpleasant tasks become yours by default.

Anyway, Grace is doing wonderfully with the potty thing. I must say that you never really notice how filthy public restrooms are until you bring your two year old into one to go potty. I can't tell you how many times I've just held her over the toilet so that she could do her business. I would honestly rather risk getting peed on than have her come anywhere near the toilet seat!

Beyond the potty thing, she is also going to 'school' now. Her daycare has a preschool at which she has learned her ABC's from start to finish and how to count all the way to eleventeen and beyond, among other important life skills. I am quite a proud poppa.

Kyle

As for me, I was fired for the first time in my life. I must say it was not quite as bad as I thought it might be. My employers, though very wealthy, were grievously deprived of that already rare commodity known as 'common sense'. And I consider it a privilege to have worked for them and learned very thoroughly how to sink a business in six months or less.

Thankfully, God was smiling on me a few months later when I was able to convince another employer that I am worth having on their payroll. Since then I have been working for Catalina Marketing Corporation. We're the guys who print out the coupons right there at the cash register when you check out. You buy Ben and Jerry's we give you a coupon for Dreyers', etc.

To put it simply, I make those coupons. Of course, it is a bit more complex than that but I can't possibly explain it in such a way as to make it the least bit entertaining. So, I will spare you the details.

And yes another year has passed and I am still not my own boss. But in this goal I am undeterred. I am convinced that as soon as I figure out that niche that will satisfy both our bank account and my soul (whether it be the coffee business, writing or something else) I'll be set. The rest is just hard work. Prayers in this regard are welcome as are suggestions.

Trouble Dog

Last but not least there's our faithful pooch Trouble. You'll notice the return address on your envelope is a P.O. Box. Yep, that's right — After a two year effort, that has included a new fence to keep her in, a new mailbox down at the street and other sundry attempts to thwart her, Trouble has finally managed to scare off the U.S. Postal Service for good. Now that's determination. She is a reminder to us all that no goal is too large.

And finally, I must come to a close. Another year has passed; A year filled with poops on the big girl potty and poops on the bathroom floor; a year of getting fired and a year of getting hired; in short another year of bitter disappointments and amazing triumphs. And another year has passed where I can honestly say with every ounce of my being, thank you for being there for me and mine. It is our friends and family who have kept our heads up during the trials and were the first to congratulate our successes. We love you all and wish you a wonderful holiday and a blessed New Year!

The Ervins—Kyle, Brynn, Grace, Isaiah and Trouble Dog

Baby Isaiah, Brynn and the New Big Sister

CHAPTER TEN
Uncommon Valor

When the United States Marines took Iwo Jima Island during World War II, Admiral Nimitz of the United States Navy had a quote that is famous among Marines. He said, "Among the men who fought on Iwo Jima, uncommon valor was a common virtue."

The same could be said of the staff of Anaheim Regional Hospital on December 2, 2009. On that day, there were many heroes. There were many feats of courage melding together with skill and knowledge that made this story possible.

Of those feats, Doctor John Eugene's open heart surgery on my wife is a remarkable example. It is a feat of surgical prowess that can be appreciated by the layman as well as any medical professional. There is no better way to explain it than to give it to you directly from his own notes of the surgery.

I have taken the liberty of explaining the procedure throughout as best I can.

PROCEDURE IN DETAIL (Truncated by the author): The patient was taken to the operating room and placed in a supine position upon the table. She still had CPR ongoing at this time and the patient was already intubated and was put to sleep with general endotracheal anesthesia. And the chest, abdomen, both grounds and both lower extremities were prepped with Chlorhexidine solution and draped.

A midline chest incision was made. Hemostasis was obtained with electrocautery. Extensive bleeding was noted as soon as we made the incision and continued through the operation. We dissected down to the sternum. The sternum was divided in the midline with the sternal saw. The sternum was retracted. Additional hemostasis was obtained with bone wax and again with electrocautery, We opened the pericardium. The right ventricle was dilated and the heart was contracting poorly, and the patient was hypotensive. A pericardial crater was created with interrupted sutures of 0 silk.

**

Brynn's heart was now exposed. Her right ventricle was blowing up like a balloon because blood could flow in but could not exit through the pulmonary arteries. They placed her on the heart-lung bypass, and soon her right ventricle decompressed.

**

SURGEON'S NOTES, continued
We placed an antegrade cardioplegia infusion cannula in the ascending aorta and secured this in place with a pursestring suture and rubber tourniquet, and connected this to the cardioplegia infusion manifold. The cross clamp was placed. Warm antegrade cardioplegia solution was followed by cold antegrade cardioplegia solution and cardiac standstill was achieved.

***

Brynn's heart was no longer trying to beat.

***

SURGEON'S NOTES, continued

We went ahead at this time and exposed the pulmonary artery and opened the pulmonary artery. The suctions were placed in the pulmonary artery and then we used ring forceps in order to explore the pulmonary arteries and begin to extract clots. We extracted thrombus from both main arteries, but it was felt that there should still be more thrombus left to account for the severity of her disease and, therefore, I opened both pleural spaces at this time and began to compress the lungs and essentially milked the lungs to try to get the clots back into the main pulmonary artery. Once we did this, we then used our ring forceps again and were able to extract larger and deeper clots from the pulmonary arteries. We then used a number 5 and then a number 4 Fogarty catheter down into both main pulmonary arteries in order to extract additional thrombus. At this point, we irrigated and we felt that we had cleaned most of the thrombus out of the pulmonary arteries. We were concerned that there might be a thrombus in the inferior vena cava.

***

The surgeon actually removed Brynn's lungs from her chest cavity and manually squeezed more clots from them. *Please, God, let them do their finest work.*

***

SURGEON'S NOTES, continued
At this point, we went and closed the pulmonary artery with a continuous horizontal mattress suture of 5-0 Prolene, followed by a continuous suture of 5-0 Prolene, and then we removed to the right atrium. We placed a pursestring suture in the superior vena cava and inserted a number 26 cannula, and secured this in place with a pursestring suture and rubber tourniquet so that we now had 2 cannulas in the right atrium. We opened the right atrium and we pulled back on the previous cannula, and we passed our Fogarty catheters and also did not extract additional clots. We checked the right atrium and the right ventricle and did not find additional clots. We went ahead and closed the atrium with a continuous horizontal mattress suture of 4-0 Prolene, followed by a continuous suture of 5-0 Prolene. At this point, we had given 2 doses of cardioplegic solution. We now gave reperfusion cardioplegic solution and the heart began beating spontaneously.

***

Brynn's heart was now beating again. They began the process of closing. In the end, she was on the cardiopulmonary bypass for sixty-three minutes.

A doctor came into the waiting room. He was an older man with silver hair and he looked exhausted after the lengthy and difficult surgery. "Gregg, is it?" he asked me.

"Uh, no. My name's Kyle."

"Oh, your shirt says Gregg." I was wearing a shirt from a company I sometimes work with, called Gregg Drilling.

"I'm Doctor Eugene; I did the surgery on your wife." He spoke haltingly as though he were searching for words and could not find them. I have to admit, I was a little set back by this first impression.

As I would get to know Dr. Eugene better over the next month, though I only saw him occasionally, I came to this conclusion about his rather odd manner—he is one of those people whose mind moves too quickly for normal mortals. His brain has moved on to the next thought long before he speaks.

"Mr. Ervin," he continued, "the good news is that she survived the surgery. They are trying to wean her off the heart-lung bypass right now. However, she was without oxygen for quite some time."

I later found out from the lead nurse who responded to the code that "quite some time" was actually ninety-five minutes. From the time the code was called (as noted on her pager) to the time Brynn was finally on cardiopulmonary bypass (as noted in the surgical notes) was over an hour and a half. For ninety-five minutes, Brynn's brain had been without oxygen.

The doctor continued, "There is no knowing what that time without oxygen has done to her higher brain functions. There is likely to be serious damage."

I was not surprised by this news. This was exactly the news that I had suspected. Even if her body survived, my Brynn was gone. She would be nothing but the shell, nothing but a beating heart. The infinitesimal amount of hope that I'd had, the candle flame that burned amongst the universe of darkness had been blown out and stood, smoking in the dark.

"Mr. Ervin." It was a nurse speaking to me now. She had short-cropped, sandy blonde hair, and penetrating blue eyes. She spoke with a slight South African accent. "We'd like to try a hypothermic treatment for your wife."

One raindrop at a time—this nurse was the lead nurse on the code team that responded to Brynn's Code Blue. Her name is Joan Strydom. She was one of the people who absolutely refused to stop trying to save Brynn. Remarkably, she was one of only two nurses in the entire hospital who had any experience with hypothermia treatment.

As we stood in the hallway, she explained to me what happens to the brain when it is without oxygen for a very long time. "There is the initial cell death. But most of the damage is due to a chain reaction—basically a wildfire in the brain. Cooling the body helps to stop that chain reaction."

The candle of hope reignited. The flame was tiny, and it was still surrounded by infinite darkness. But it was not out. The nurse went on to explain that there were some risks with the treatment. The greatest of these was exsanguination (known colloquially as "bleeding out").

Cooling her body would reduce its ability to heal itself from the surgeries, and she might still die from blood loss. This risk was so great that hypothermic treatment is actually contraindicated after surgery. In fact, the doctors had not wanted to proceed with this treatment. Joan, however, showing her own uncommon valor, pushed for the treatment.

From my standpoint, it was not a difficult decision. I instantly simplified the possibilities in my mind. She had been without oxygen to her brain for over an hour. The insult to her body was such that, no matter what I decided, the greatest probability was that she would die. If we played it safe and kept everything "as is," Brynn could have an okay chance of living, but would almost certainly remain in a persistent vegetative state. If I chose to allow them to try this hypothermic treatment, there was a greater chance that she could die, there was also a good chance that she would remain in a persistent vegetative state, but there was a candle's flame of hope that her brain could be saved. My Brynn without her mind is not my Brynn.

"Where do I sign?"

"There's something else you need to know. Normally, for this treatment we would use a piece of high-tech equipment to maintain and monitor the hypothermic state. This hospital does not have that equipment. However, we can use cooling blankets."

"Where do I sign?"

My approval was not the only approval they needed though. That night, countless members of the hospital's upper management were consulted. Entire careers would be on the line based on this decision. In a display of institutional courage that I will forever marvel at, they all chose to move forward. They did what needed to be done to give my wife a chance.

***

Once it was apparent that she would make it through surgery, I decided to have the kids head home. I was strangely confident that Brynn would not die. I was *not* optimistic about her recovery, but I wasn't worried about her dying. She had always been strong—so strong. She had delivered three children, all naturally without the benefits of epidurals. She could survive a little open heart surgery. But her brain—what was going to happen to her brain?

My parents took the kids home and we moved into another waiting room in the cardiovascular unit. By this time, I had been in a state of extreme anxiety for about six hours. My mind's capacity for memory failed, and all

I can recall is sitting in that room. I can't remember who was there. I just remember sitting there.

Eventually, somebody came in and walked me back to see my wife.

Christmas Letter, 2005

Hello Again, Everybody,

Another year has passed. 365 days of dirty diapers, hugs, annoying alarm clocks, belly laughs, and so much more. We're another year older. We've acquired another year's worth of aches and pains and, God willing, another year's worth of wisdom. (Though in my own case, I have some doubts).

Nevertheless, I once again find myself ingesting copious amounts of coffee, doing unknown damage to my internal organs, desperately trying to write something even remotely interesting. But never mind that... It's Christmas!!! A time to celebrate, spread joy and love, and all that stuff. And who cares if I've developed a caffeine tick in my left eye? It's a small price to pay to let our friends and family know that we're thinking of them. Pardon me for a moment—I have to pee.

Right then, back to business—The Ervin Family, 2005. Where do I begin? I guess I'll start with the youngest and work my way up.

Isaiah

Okay—a note to all prospective parents out there: *when you have to make a song to remember how to spell your own son's name, there's a problem*. On that note, should any of you biblically challenged individuals (like myself) misspell his name in the future, you are automatically forgiven. Those of you who have had a religious education, however, there is no excuse for you and we will wrap your knuckles with a ruler.

Isaiah, however, doesn't seem to mind that we've strapped him with such a *vowellicious* name. It may be another three years before he can pronounce it though. You see, unlike his loquacious older sister, Isaiah hasn't yet found much use for the English language. In fact, he has thus far limited his communication skills to a series of grunts, growls, and whines for the most part. On the occasions that he desires to nurse, however, he will resort to a somewhat panicked panting through his nose. It sounds like something you might expect from an obscene phone call, and never fails to elicit a laugh from his old man.

I should be careful how much I make fun of him though. He's a big boy and is destined to out-grow his old man considerably. Not to mention the fact that he moves like the wind. He's been walking since the tender age of nine months and hasn't stopped yet.

That's reason number one that Brynn and I have been forced to re-babyproof the entire house. We just can't keep track of him. Besides that, he is much more of an "experimenter" than Grace was. He wants to know how everything works. And when I say everything, I mean every-thing! From electrical sockets to telephones to toilet paper rolls. Ah... you laugh now, but wait until you're stranded on the pot with no TP in sight. We'll see whose laughing then.

Grace

As for our beautiful daughter, I think she may have a future in law enforcement. It has been more than once that her parents have been caught short breaking their own rules, including but not limited to such offenses as the use of *potty words*, hitting (yes, my wife occasionally gives me a well-deserved smack in the head), and the most grievous offense of all, walking outside the white lines of the cross walk. I've spent more time on "time out" than she has this year.

She is also learning to spell, which I'm not sure is such a good thing. Brynn and I find ourselves needing to get more and more creative as to how we tell secrets because she's starting to decipher what we're saying. Spanish doesn't work, either, because her Spanish vocabulary is getting close to exceeding my own. Curse you, Dora the Explorer!

Beyond her NSA-worthy code-breaking skills, she has discovered a love of running... especially in what her Auntie Alisa has dubbed her *fastest running shoes*. This is, of course, an activity that we promote because it helps to deplete her almost inexhaustible energy reserves.

Luckily, I won't have to worry about her much longer though. You see, she's getting married to her boyfriend Jake. He's a young man from her preschool and he has apparently taken Superman's place as her new beau. God bless you, Jake... and good luck.

Brynn

Oh, yes, and on to my wife. Sure, I tease her mercilessly, but she is truly my better half... Better looking, better smelling, better dressed, better singer, better dancer, better housekeeper, and the list goes on. Not only that, but she also puts up with me and all my shenanigans.

It's true that I'm not known for my incredibly brilliant life decisions. Some might even call me "reckless" as I often give my heart reign over my head (mostly because it works better). But I have to say, the day I got down on one knee in front of her was pretty freakin' brilliant on my part. Whether her saying yes was equally brilliant on her part is yet to be determined.

Kyle

Speaking of following my heart (or being reckless... whichever you prefer), I left that ridiculously mind-numbing coupon job in order to pursue the writing thing. I have faith that it is my calling, but I also have to be honest. It has been an unbelievably miserable experience. Finding yourself with more bills than money is a nausea-inducing predicament I wouldn't wish on anyone. This is especially true when you have two young children for which you are responsible. But it is in such predicaments that we get to learn how truly blessed we are, for it is the family and friends that surround us which are our true blessings, and in the past months I have come to consider myself the most blessed man on earth.

So how else can I repay the kindness, love, and generosity other than wishing equal blessings upon you and yours. We love you all.

Merry Christmas and Happy New Year
The Ervins—Kyle, Brynn, Grace, Isaiah, and Trouble Dog.

CHAPTER ELEVEN
Sleeping Beauty

Anaheim Regional Medical Center, December 2, 2009, sometime after surgery

There she was, my wife, lying motionless on the hospital bed. Just barely visible beneath her hospital gown was the evidence of her surgery. Her chest was stained with iodine, and a foot-long bandage covered the wound from just below her collarbone down to her stomach. Her rib cage rose and fell in unison with the rhythmic mechanical pumping of the ventilator. Protruding from her stomach were three tubes running into a plastic catch basin that measured how much blood she was losing.

Behind and above her, multiple IV bags and their associated pumps pushed countless drugs and multiple units of blood into her system to keep her alive. Spread over her was a simple cooling blanket trying to do the job of keeping her core temperature hovering around ninety degrees. It was not the perfect solution. It was, in fact, a rather archaic way to manage her hypothermic state. But I had to hope it would work. What other choice was there?

Beyond that, two large flexible tubes were draped over the left side of her bed, running from the ventilator to a "y" union and then down through her throat to her lungs. I was terrified to get anywhere near the machines—terrified that I might knock one and cause it to fail. I gave them a wide berth, walking over to the right side of her bed. The IV line and all of the electrical monitoring cables ran on this side, and I was still terrified, but I had to get close to her. The nurse was kind enough to lower the bedrail for me. I picked up her limp hand and sandwiched it between my two hands, blinked the moisture from my eyes, and sniffled the snot that began to pour from my nose.

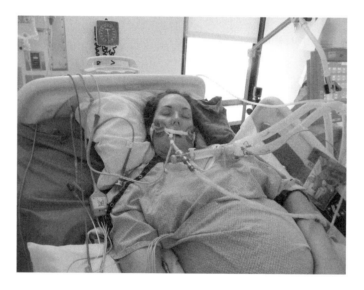

Brynn in Coma

"You're so cold." Her hand felt as if it had just been shoved in a bucket of ice. "You hate being cold," I said to her, my voice shaking. "You would be so mad at me right now." I was just able to get the last words out before I was crying again.

She, of course, could not feel anything, but I could not help feeling that I was somehow failing her by allowing her to be so cold. Since that day on the Golden Gate Bridge, it had been my job to keep her warm. For eight years, whenever her feet were cold in bed, she pressed them against my much warmer legs. We would fall asleep in a sort of marital symbiosis; I warmed her feet, she kept me cool under the heavy covers.

As I stood next to her hospital bed, holding her hand, I wanted to climb into the bed with her and feel her feet become warm as they pressed up against my legs. I wanted to fix it. I wanted to make it right. I could not. I wanted to stay with her all night. I could not. I had three children at home who also needed me. And for the first time I felt the horrible pull—the constant strain that accompanied my need to be in many places at once—a wife in the CVU, a newborn son in the NICU, and three children at home, all in desperate need of my attention.

There was nothing else I could do. In a way it was a great blessing to know this and to understand it. I could do nothing but pray for her. So I did. I prayed that the cooling was doing its job of saving her brain, and then I said good night to my wife. Then I walked out into the empty halls of the hospital and told God that if I saw him walking down the street, I'd punch him straight in the face.

This would symbolize my relationship with "the man upstairs" for the coming struggle—prayerful, thankful, and unbelievably pissed off, all at the same time. Unknown to me, and despite my anger, while I was visiting with my wife, God was still busy moving oceans.

Among the many phone calls made that night by the staff of Anaheim Regional was one made by the manager of the cardiovascular unit—*Let them be amazing.* Her cousin is the CFO at Mission Hospital in Mission Viejo. Mission Hospital is actually a competing hospital with Anaheim Regional. But Mission has the high-tech equipment for monitoring and maintaining the hypothermic state. It is called the Arctic Sun. The CVU manager told her cousin about this mother of four that had suffered a massive pulmonary embolism and subsequent cardiopulmonary arrest.

In an act of heroic cooperation Mission Hospital agreed to allow Anaheim Regional to use the equipment—*Let them do their finest work.*

Joan Strydom, the nurse who had suggested the treatment to me, after already working over fourteen hours, drove the sixty-mile round trip to pick up the machine. Unbelievably, a 40,000-dollar piece of equipment was put in the back of her car with nothing more than the sarcastic admonition, "You break it, you buy it."

Experts in hypothermia from Mission Hospital would also provide twenty-four-hour on-call support, giving the Anaheim Regional staff the advice and information they needed to treat Brynn. Beyond that, the nurses at Anaheim Regional needed the courage and mental fortitude to treat a patient using a technique new to them that might cause their patient to bleed to death. It took many brave nurses and two courageous hospitals to give Brynn a chance.

***

After leaving Brynn's bedside, I went home, arriving around ten o'clock. My parents were still awake, waiting for me. Grace, Isaiah, and Noah had fallen asleep together in our bed. I watched them for a moment, sleeping so peacefully together. I envied them. I knew I would not be sleeping for quite some time.

I wrote an email to my colleagues at Vironex, the environmental company where I worked, explaining that I would be taking an indefinite leave of absence. I knew we couldn't afford for me to take an extended leave, but I also knew that my absolute highest priority at that time was for me to be a 100 percent full-time husband and father. Paying the bills was a very distant second.

Then, knowing I needed my strength for the coming days, I crawled into bed with my three children for what I expected to be a night of lying in the dark with my eyes closed, resting my body if not my mind. You see, since I was a small child, I've often had difficulty getting to sleep. My mind can become a runaway freight train of thought, impossible to slow down to speeds conducive to sleep. Over the years I've developed techniques for slowing it down, usually employing some form of meditation. Sometimes I can hijack the train so that it will take me to imaginary places. But I doubted any of that would work that night. There was simply too much going on in my head.

I lay there in the dark, taking in the warmth of my children's small bodies, listening to their breathing. Grace's tiny little snore was dominating the lighter breaths of her two younger brothers. I smiled at the thought that she is the boss in sleep just as she is the boss in play. I listened to my children, closed my eyes, and reached out into the darkness behind them for my Brynn. I have a wonderfully vivid imagination and so I wasn't surprised to find her there. What I was surprised by was how real she was. Her whole personality seemed to radiate toward me from the darkness. In that moment, I absolutely believed she was there with me, and to this day, I tell you with absolute certainty that she was there—with me.

I talked to her at length about things I can't remember. Mostly, I asked her to come back to us. Her presence in the darkness calmed me and somehow, some way, I was able to fall asleep for two hours or so and get the rest I would need to take me through the next day.

I slept very soundly until about midnight when Brynn's sister, Katie, brought me the phone. I had been sleeping so deeply that I hadn't heard it ring. Katie was panicked, because it was the hospital on the other end. She was certain they were calling to tell us Brynn had not survived the night.

Fortunately, they were only calling to get verbal permission to use the hypothermia treatment. In all the confusion and craziness and paper signing, I had not actually signed the consent for that crucial treatment.

After the reawakening, I tossed and turned until about 4:00 a.m. when I finally decided to get out of bed. I went out to the living room couch and began a morning tradition that took me through the darkest days. I got on the computer and played a couple of games of solitaire. I was contemplating how best to divulge the news of this tragedy to those who love my wife and my family. I knew I couldn't do it by phone. There were too many people to notify and I couldn't imagine telling the story again more than once. Then, in a stroke of inspired genius I got onto my Facebook account and entered the following as my status...

> Yesterday, Brynn suffered a pulmonary embolism. A blood clot broke free from her legs and fully blocked her pulmonary artery. She had emergency surgery. Unfortunately, she was without oxygen for quite some time. She made it through surgery well but is currently in an induced coma and an artificial state of hypothermia. We have plenty of help but as always we would be greatly appreciative of your prayers–Kyle

I remember it taking me several drafts to get all the pertinent information into 450 characters or less. It was slightly frustrating but I knew, instinctively, that it was the single best method for sharing news of Brynn's situation with those that love her.

It was as simple as that. Twenty minutes online and then I signed off, and I prepared to go for a walk, something I often do to clear my mind. Little did I know, that single post, like the solitary match that lights a bonfire, hit the dry tinder of hundreds of faithful people, lighting a bonfire of prayer and meditation that would eventually be seen all over the entire earth.

Christmas Letter, 2006

Dear People to whom I could not be bothered to send this prior to Christmas,

So, I've been reviewing my performance reviews from upper management regarding my Christmas letters of years past. Overall, I must say the comments were pretty good. However, I did get poor marks for punctuality. In fact, I've only managed to get the letter out in time for Christmas once—MY BAD.

Anyway, in an effort to impress upper management with my willingness to make efforts towards better performance, I have presented them with an idea on how to improve my timeliness. The idea is more or less as follows: Change the title from "The Ervin Christmas Letter" to "The Ervin Year-end Letter."

Needless to say, upper management is extremely pleased with the concept and have touted my "new paradigm/out of the box" thinking. I told them I could think like that all the time if they wanted. All they'd have to do is get rid of the coffeepot and replace it with Guinness on tap. I've since been promoted to V.P.

The only problem with that is I now have to get this letter done super quick because I've got an eleven o'clock tee time—so here it goes.

First and foremost, we have another Ervin inbound. ETA is February 3rd. All indications are that it's another boy. But "all indications" is a single ultrasound done when he was about the size of a newborn squirrel. And the fact that we are having an impossible time coming up with a boy's name is beginning to cast doubt as to the validity of said ultrasound. I guess you'll just have to wait 'til the next year-end letter to find out for sure. Don't you just love cliff-hangers? Just kidding! I'm sure there will be a birth announcement. Let's see, the kid's coming in February so you should receive an announcement around July—maybe August.

As for the little tykes that aren't in Momma's belly, they are getting along famously. In fact, just last night, Grace was playing house and she let Isaiah play with her. Grace was the mom, her doll was the baby, Elmo was the daddy, and Isaiah got to be the dog. Now if that isn't sibling love, I don't know what is.

Beyond playing house, they are both very busy doing their part to maintain the trade deficit with China. Together they have managed to accumulate roughly six metric tons of McDonald's Happy Meal toys. Quite an accomplishment for ones so young.

Gracie is learning to spell. This development has had the unfortunate consequence of destroying the "Mother-Father secret code" that we've enjoyed for the past four years. We discovered this when Brynn asked me if I wanted to take the kids to the P-A-R-K and Grace shouts out, "Yes! Yes! Can we go to the park!?" Brynn and I are now taking night classes in the Navajo language.

Now, spelling P-A-R-K is one thing. But you'll understand why I was pleasantly surprised the other night when we were in the car and Gracie says to me "Daddy! Daddy! I can spell toilet paper. Want to hear?"

I'm thinking to myself, *Whoa! That's pretty cool.* That's two words with a diphthong thrown in. So I tell her I'd love to hear her spell it. She obliges and starts spelling in her very methodical way, "T" (pregnant pause as she thinks very hard as to what the next letter is), "P," "T.P. spells toilet paper." I laughed so hard, I almost crashed the car.

Isaiah isn't quite spelling yet. In fact he's only been talking for about seven months. Mom was beginning to worry that he had bumped his head one too many times while learning to walk. I told her not to worry because he's got the Ervin skull, which is approximately six times denser than a normal skull.

Sure enough, he started to talk. Some favorite phrases are:

Gracie, share!

Gracie no share, Dada!

Gracie hit me, Dada! (Which is immediately followed by, "He started it!")

Poo-poo head (Yeah, he picked that one up at school)

And the favorite of two-year-olds every-where...NO!

He's your typical two-year-old boy in so many other ways as well. He loves playing with trains and balls, *wearing his sister's clothes*, playing Buzz Lightyear on the couch, *putting on makeup with Auntie Carole*, and fighting the monsters under the bed. He makes his daddy proud...*except when he wears Grace's Daddy's Little Princess' shirt in public.*

Brynn is, of course, doing her best imperson-ation of a hippity hop ball, and looking as beau-tiful as ever doing it. She is still teaching, though we've begun to toy with the idea of having her home. Unfortunately, the economics aren't look-ing too good right now. It's too bad we're not the US government. Then we could just deficit spend and lay the debt off on our grandchildren. I'm sure they wouldn't mind.

As for me, it's been a pretty good year pro-fessionally. I'm working for a company called Vironex. They do environmental field services. I'm not going to tell you what that is so that I'll have something to talk about at parties still. Suffice it to say the job keeps me active and outdoors and is continually putting my problem solving skills to the test. To put it bluntly, it's the perfect gig for a guy with a *slight* case of attention deficit disor-der. By the way, has anybody seen my wallet?

Speaking of wallets, and the lack of anything to fill them, we acquired another cost center this year in the form of a new puppy. He already cost me over 200 dollars in vet bills when he decid-ed to devour a one pound chocolate bar. We breathed a sigh of relief when we brought him home from the vet safe and sound only to have him devour another two boxes of Christmas chocolates about one hour later. Luckily he was still vomiting from the ipecac the vet had given him from his previous poisoning, so I didn't have to worry about a dead dog; I only had to worry about numerous pools of activated charcoal and chocolate vomit that decorated my floors.

Anyway, Grace got to name him and so chose a name that she could spell easily: B-I-N-

G-O and Bingo was his name-O! He's been a great addition to our home. Even Trouble welcomed him without too much chagrin. She was sure to teach him how things are done in the Ervin household. And on the flip side, boy did he bring out the puppy in her.

Unfortunately, their friendship was not to be a long one. Trouble's health took a real bad turn in July as she lost her eyesight, her mobility, and about thirty pounds in a month's time. In August I had to take one of my best friends in the world to the vet and hold her head as I watched her pass into the next world. It was extremely tough, but it was even tougher trying to explain to Grace and Isaiah where Trouble was, and why Daddy was crying. There's no doubt that Trouble Dog will be sorely missed (though perhaps not by members of the United States Postal Service). We love ya, Trouble girl.

As you can tell, 2006 has been a year jam packed full of miraculous gains and tragic losses. And once again we consider ourselves incredibly blessed to have so many wonderful people in our lives who have cheered us in our highs and likewise lifted us out of our lows. To put it plainly, You all Rock! And we love you.

Merry Christmas and Happy New Year
Sincerely, The Ervin Clan: Kyle, Brynn, Grace, Isaiah, "No Name," and Bingo

CHAPTER TWELVE
Benjamin Button

Anaheim Regional Medical Center, December 3, 2009

On December 3, 2009, the woman I had gotten down on one knee for over eight years prior was in a medically induced coma and an artificial state of hypothermia with an infinitesimal probability for survival. The son she had borne not two days before was facing his own struggle for life, three floors above her in the neonatal intensive care unit.

It was a Thursday, but the only reason I know this is because I can look back on a calendar. Things like days of the week or even months of the year were not registering in my head any more. Morning, noon, and night were about all I could manage. Oh, and the ever important "shift change." Nurses would change shifts at 7:00 a.m. and 7:00 p.m., and this meant we were not allowed to visit. That was it. That was all my head could hold.

The day before, in all the commotion, I had somehow strained the Achilles tendon on my right foot. I had probably done it running up and down the hospital stairs. It hadn't hurt at all on Wednesday. On Thursday it felt like someone had kicked me in the back of the foot in a soccer game. I was limping quite badly, and so I hobbled into the hospital sometime after shift change.

I mentioned before that I do not like hospitals. They

all smell of antibiotic cleaners, they are all over-lit with fluorescent lighting, and they all have institutional paint schemes that I'm sure are designed to calm but have the exact opposite effect on me. Having the love of my life and our newest child both in life-or-death struggles inside a hospital was a very difficult situation.

As soon as I walked through the doors, Fear started doing his thing again. He began tightening around my chest. The further I went into the building, the stronger his grip became. The fact that the condition of my wife and son were already known throughout the hospital did not help. I approached the guard desk and for reasons I didn't understand, my heart was thudding in my chest. *Is he going to ask me who I am? Is he going to ask me who I am visiting?*

I still wore my hospital-issued "Father" bracelet. It was plastic and decorated with rubber duckies. I waved that at him and was utterly relieved when he simply waved me on through.

I walked down the hall to the CVU waiting room where there was a phone on the wall. As I approached the phone, the same fear I felt with the security guard welled up within me. I was afraid to pick up the phone. It was then that I finally understood the fear. I was afraid to let anybody know who I was.

As soon as I said the words, "This is Kyle Ervin to see Brynn Ervin," I would be found out. I would be *THAT GUY—the one with the wife who was dying and the son in the NICU.* I didn't want to be *that guy.*

I was *that guy,* though. I dialed the CVU extension, told them who I was, and they buzzed me in.

Behind the door was a maze of hallways that lead in one direction to ICUs (intensive care units) 1 and 2 and in the other direction to the CVU (cardiovascular unit) and the CVOU (cardiovascular observation unit). It would take me several days to learn my way around them.

Luckily, the CVU was in the far northeast corner of the maze, so I just walked in that general direction. Brynn was in room 146. It was the first room visible as you enter the unit.

I walked past the desk, greeting whoever was sitting there, and went on into her room. By this time, the Arctic Sun machine was at the foot of her bed—an ever present sentry ensuring that her core body temperature was maintained at that critical ninety degrees.

I said "Good morning" to my wife, noticing that one of her nurses had taken the time and effort to French braid her hair, "You look beautiful."

I found out a couple days later that the nurses, agreeing with my assessment, had already nicknamed her Sleeping Beauty.

I made a point to get past my fear of the IV lines and learned how to put the bedrail down for myself. I gave her a kiss on her forehead, leaving my face close to hers so I could breathe in her scent. She smelled like my Brynn, only flatter somehow, as though she were a bottle of champagne that had lost its effervescence. I thought how odd it was that I found her scent so intoxicating, and yet I could not help but to take it in. I stood there, leaning over her, inhaling deeply. This was the beginning of my fascination with her scent.

I sat down in the chair next to her bed and watched the monitor that had her every vital sign displayed: temperature, respirations, heart rate, oxygen saturation, blood pressure.

I was beginning to settle in, sipping on my cup of coffee, when an alarm went off. I jumped out of my chair, expecting nurses to come flying into the room. When nobody did, I went out into the main area of the CVU to try to find someone.

"An alarm is going off!" a sense of panic creeping into my voice as I told a nurse who was doing something behind the counter.

She looked up from her work, totally unperturbed. "Yes, one of your wife's IV drips is running low." Her tone was nonchalant but not condescending. "I'll tell her nurse."

I limped back to her room, feeling a little embarrassed but beginning to employ the classic rationalization, *How was I supposed to know?*

Shortly after the alarm, I figured it was time for a break from the intensity of her room so I leaned over her bed and told her, "I'm going to go upstairs and visit our son and see how he's doing. I love you, baby. I'll be back soon."

I limped out to the waiting room and told the friends and family accumulated there that I was headed upstairs to see Anthony. As expected with that announcement, I picked up quite an entourage. Eight or nine of us made the trip.

For reasons unknown to me, hospitals tend to be giant multi-storied labyrinths, and Anaheim Regional was no different. The day before, during the crisis, somebody showed me where to go every step of the way. Fortunately, I actually remembered the path we had taken from the postpartum area. Unfortunately, it was the convoluted route that retraced our steps, only in reverse. I started at the CVU, led the group past the operating room, around the corner past radiology, and finally to the elevator.

"Where are we going?" somebody asked.

"We're trying to get to the elevators. This is the only way I know."

I would spend many hours walking the halls of that hospital. Within a couple of days I learned better ways from the CVU to the NICU, and within weeks I became a master of the labyrinth. I spotted other people walking around with confused looks on their faces, reading the signs for directions, and I pointed them to the right way.

That day, however, our entourage made it to the elevators by my convoluted path, and then took the elevator up to the third floor. I walked back to the NICU where there was a phone on the wall—another phone. Again, Fear gripped me.

I am that guy, *and I better just get used to it.*

I called back. There was a window at the wall phone that looked inside the NICU to the reception desk and the nurse who answered the phone.

"Kyle Ervin to see Anthony Ervin."

"Oh, yes, come on in." She walked over to the door and opened it for me. "We're so very sorry about your wife," she said, as I walked through the door. "How is she doing?"

It was a simple question, and well intended. Despite knowing that, I felt anger well up inside me. It was anger at having to come up with an answer to a question that I did not want to think about. And for such a simple question, it was a very difficult answer.

She's in a coma, in critical condition, and she could die from exsanguination at any minute was the truth, but seemed a harsh answer for someone who was just trying to be nice. And though I was angry at being asked, I knew it was an irrational, misplaced anger. The person asking was simply trying to show concern and did not deserve my ire. This was just part of being *that guy.* So I said as matter-of-factly as I could manage, "All things considered, she's doing pretty well. She's in an induced coma and artificial state of hypothermia. We won't know much for a while."

"Well, if there is anything we can do for you or your family, please let us know."

"I will. Thank you."

She showed me the small sink where I was to

thoroughly wash my hands whenever I entered. It had a foot pedal to turn on the water, and I scrubbed my hands up to my elbows with antibacterial soap. I remember feeling guilty because I was not able to keep all the water in the sink. I left a puddle on the floor at my feet when I was done.

"Sorry about the mess," I said as I dried my hands.

"Oh, don't worry. That's nothing compared to most," she replied, and then took me back to see my son.

I could feel the tension in the NICU. I could feel the eyes of the nurses on me as I walked—*that guy*. Nobody, not even these professional nurses, knew how to treat *that guy*. It took some getting used to.

Everywhere I went, people treated me as though I was a bomb about to go off. In fact, one of the hardest things I would have to figure out in the next few days was how to put other people at ease with me and my situation. I came to count on my sense of humor heavily in this regard.

The nurse who walked me back was doing her best to break the tension. "He's doing very well. He's already off the supplemental oxygen."

"That's great!" I replied. "So his lungs are doing well." Lung development is the biggest concern with preemies, and I wanted them to know that I had some knowledge about his situation.

"Yes, his lungs are working great," she continued. "He needs to put on some weight, though. We call him Benjamin Button 'cause he's so wrinkled he looks like a little old man," she joked, referring to the recent Brad Pitt movie about the man who lived his life in reverse. And Anthony did look like a little old man.

I joked back with the nurse, "That's fine so long as he ends up looking like Brad Pitt." The nurses around me laughed and, with that, the tension was broken and I was able to look at my son without it clouding my view.

As a child, long before I had met the woman of my dreams, and long before I had even considered having children of my own, my mom bought my sister and I matching Madame Alexander dolls. They are the dolls with the eyes that open and close depending on whether they are upright or lying down. Strangely, for a boy of that era, mine became one of my favorite toys.

The first time I saw my son after watching him be whisked away after his birth, he was roughly the same size as my childhood toy. Just like my doll, as he lay there, his eyes were closed. He was separated from the world by a bubble of plastic called an incubator. Tiny wire-thin ribs were easily visible beneath his skin and on them was stuck a red heart-shaped lead to the electrocardiogram. His right hand was wrapped in gauze, protecting the site of his first IV. The "preemie" diaper was too big for his body.

He had nothing in the way of muscle or body fat. He was a tiny skeleton with skin around it, skin that hung in wrinkled folds about his bones like a suit three sizes too big. The only places his skin was not wrinkled were the spots where translucent tape that held the IV in place kept it flat and artificially smooth. I remember looking at that tape, and all I could think of was how much it would hurt when they had to take it off. I wanted to protect him from all of this pain, all of this discomfort but, once again, there was nothing I could do.

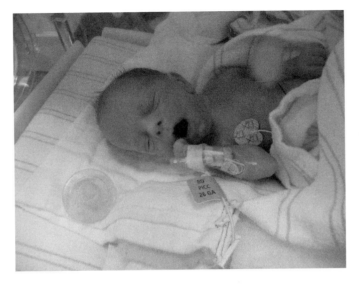

Anthony in NICU

There are those who say we are in control of our own destiny. They imagine that we can control every aspect of our lives. To those people, I have to say, "You are categorically wrong."

There were aspects of my situation that I could control. But the outcome was entirely out of my hands. It was like being on a train heading for a gorge where the bridge was out. I was hoping the breaks would stop me, but there was nothing I could do to slow down the train. I just sat in my seat and prayed.

Anthony was so small and apparently fragile that I hesitated to hold him. Seeing the hesitation written all over my face, the nurse took him from the incubator. "Here, Dad, hold your son," she said to me, a tone of command in her voice, as she handed him over, giving me no chance to back out. I felt as if I might break him. But knowing how important human touch was for him I got past my fear and took him into my arms.

As I held my newest son in my hands, his head about the size of an apple, I was surprised, frightened, and ashamed by my own emotional detachment. The word *burden* floated through my mind. The only complete thought I was able to muster as I held him was, *How am I going to care for you without your mother?*

The entourage that accompanied me was waiting at the large window of the NICU outside in the hallway. I hid my shame and fear behind my best fake smile and held him up so that everybody could see him. I was aware of their presence behind the glass, but it was just the two of us together—*that guy* and his tiny baby boy, *Benjamin Button.*

Grace and Isaiah Meet Their Brother

Christmas Letter, 2007

WARNING! PARENTAL DISCRETION ADVISED.
CHILDREN UNDER THE AGE OF 13 MUST BE
ACCOMPANIED BY AN ADULT

Hello All! And welcome to another addition of the Ervin Family Year-end Letter!

I will start off on a positive noting that we are now ten months into the state of being outnumbered by our children and all five of us are still alive. Granted, alcohol consumption amongst the two grownups has increased somewhat. But we never drink to get drunk. Well at least never at the same time.

One unexpected consequence of having given birth to and raising three children, though, is that Brynn seems to be experiencing noticeable cognitive degradation. In layman's terms: the woman can't remember squat. Now it's true that I may have been similarly affected, but as I've always been somewhat forgetful, it's less noticeable.

Anyway, there are certain advantages to having a forgetful wife. One upside, for instance, is that our entire DVD collection is brand new to her. And that saves me a ton of dough. The downside of that upside is that I'm going to have to endure *Pride and Prejudice* another 432 times before my wife gets tired of it again. Oh, did I forget to mention that she has both the BBC version AND the Keira Knightly version? Oh, how I suffer.

But the benefits of Brynn's LFIMDD (large family induced memory deficit disorder) far outweigh the deficits. Mostly it just helps to keep me out of the doghouse. For instance, on occasions when

I might have gone a little bit overboard on a trip to Home Depot, all I have to say is, "But, honey, we discussed it. You thought it would be a great idea to get a Dewalt 12-inch Compound Miter Saw. Don't you remember?"

"We did?" she'll reply, visibly searching her memory banks for the conversation.

"Yes. Remember, it was when the baby was crying, and Grace spilled her Cheerios on the floor."

"Oh—really? Well—okay."

And that's that. It's like living with that guy from *Memento*.

Beyond her memory issues she has traded out her once-preferred Chardonnay for Jack and Coke (This is where Isaiah might interject with "Don't throw Momma under da bus, Dada." But, really, what fun would that be?).

This change in drinks has had multiple benefits for me, first of which is that I don't get hassled for buying whiskey anymore. The other benefit ought not to be discussed in mixed company.

I do find it ironic, though, that my sweet, innocent Brynn was introduced to the "hard stuff" by two of her teaching colleagues, Mr. Bean and Mrs. Esparza. It begs the question of how many of my teachers I drove to the bottle as a youngster. My guess is, more than one.

But despite the stress at home and work, she somehow still manages to be an excellent wife and amazing mother. My blessings grow every year I'm married to her.

As for the little Ervins, I'll start with Isaiah since he has the most recent notable achievement. As of November 18, 2007, he is officially potty trained! Now, keep in mind that Dad's been lobbying for him to put his diapers away for the past six months. But he would not budge. Oh sure, he knew how and even when to use the potty, but he was loathe to give up the convenience of diapers. It was like trying to negotiate with a miniature Ahmadinajad protecting his nuclear ambitions.

It was mom that finally got him to make concessions. Let me tell you, the U.N. ain't got nothing on Brynn. Together, they somehow arranged a deal that, when he turned three and was officially a big boy, he would put on big-boy undies. He woke up on his birthday, put on his Spider Man tighty whities and hasn't worn a diaper since. Could you imagine a world in which all politicians were as true to their word???

Okay, now for the PG-13 part—for those of you with more "refined" (read prudish) sensibilities you may want to skip these next couple paragraphs. Just know that what you are about to skip is frickin' hilarious.

BEGIN CENSORED MATERIAL

Isaiah, as all members of the male sex eventually do, has discovered his penis. And, like all members of the male sex before him, also discovered that it is not just a tool for peeing. This, of course, has led to many awkward moments. A prime example was the time Brynn was changing his diaper in the living room and had to explain to him that playing with his penis in the living room was inappropriate.

His deadpan response, "What about my balls, Momma? Can I play with my balls?"

And while I'm in the process of embarrassing my defenseless three-year-old, I might as well mention his mammary fascination. That's right, that boy loves boobs. Now he has a definite preference for his mother's but, as many female friends and family members will attest, any boob will do in a pinch.

END OF CENSORED MATERIAL

Speaking of pinching, the newest member of the Ervin Clan, little baby Noah, has taken to getting his parents' attention by clenching our soft fleshy parts with his chimpanzee grip to the point of drawing blood. If that excruciating tactic doesn't work, he puts his four new incisors to work. My poor wife is the most frequent recipient of such attentions. Nary a day goes by that our small home doesn't echo with my wife's shrieking voice, "OW! NO BITING!"

Like his brother and father before him, baby Noah seems to think that a rakish grin is all that's necessary to win over his mother after such transgressions. He's young and has much to learn. Isaiah and I know that it is a testament to Brynn's love that he still maintains full function of all his limbs.

Baby Noah, Brynn and the New Big Brother and Big Sister

I've thought of hobbling the little tyke myself, but for very different reasons. You see, like his elder siblings, baby Noah is an early walker. He took his first steps at about nine months, and is now bipedal about half the time. I am taking this as definitive proof that God enjoys tormenting me.

As for the eldest, Grace is now officially a real kindergartner. She had a bit of a rough start being at a new school with all new kids, but she has managed superbly. I'm astonished by the amount of homework she's given, though. To her credit she works on it diligently, much more so than her old man ever did. Oh, you say you want evidence of her academic achievement?

How's this: "Daddy, I know what c—r—a—p spells. It spells crap!"

My response of course…"Oh, s—h—i—t!"

Beyond her spelling prowess, she is also an excellent big sister. She comforts her brothers when they're upset. She fetches diapers. And she's only dropped Noah off the couch once.

Needless to say, life in the Ervin household is a bit crazy. Our total mess-making potential far outstrips our mess-cleaning capabilities. Hence, the house is pretty much in a perpetual state of untidiness. Basically, if you want to feel good about your own housekeeping abilities, just come visit our house. You'll have enough material for months' worth of self-righteous indignation. It's a sacrifice I'm willing to make to help my friends and family to boost their egos a bit.

If it weren't for Nana Holderness, I don't know what we'd do. In fact, I'm going to start calling my mother-in-law Mrs. Weasley (if you haven't read Harry Potter all I can say is, GET WITH IT, MAN!).

Anyway, she's got to be pullin' a *scourgio* charm on our house when she's watching our children two days a week. It's the only way I can explain her ability to clean our kitchen, and living room, while simultaneously watching all three kids.

The only other explanation that I can think of (And believe me I've considered doing it myself more than once) is locking all three of them in the bathroom while cleaning. But I've interrogated the kids and they corroborate Nana's story. So it's got to be magic. I wonder if I can get her to use that wand on my French doors, seeing as I've had them installed for almost a year and have yet to finish painting them.

And now, I suppose it's my turn. For those that don't already know, I am officially a cancer survivor. Yes, all that fun in the sun in my youth came back to haunt me in the form of a potentially deadly freckle. It was my dear wife that saved my butt with her persistent requests that I go see the dermatologist. I finally relented only to find out that the freckle she had been bugging me for over a year to have checked (that I was convinced was nothing) turned out to be melanoma. I WILL NEVER LIVE THIS DOWN!!! I've since had the offending freckle removed and have a nice four-inch scar and a little divot in my arm to takes its place.

It's easy, now, to look back on my brush with the "C" word with levity. But there was about a month there when I didn't know whether cancer cells had found their way into my lymphatic system, possibly poisoning the rest of my body. And I would be lying to say that I wasn't scared out of my mind. The fear of not seeing my children grow to adulthood and have children of their own was suddenly an all-too-real possibility. That and the thought of leaving my wife with three young ones and a mortgage was more than enough to keep me tossing and turning well into the night.

And then came the deluge of phone calls from our family and friends. I have to be honest, I made Brynn answer these, because I am emotionally incapable of dealing with so many people caring about me so much. But it was exactly those phone calls that brought me the first peaceful night's sleep of my ordeal. Because it was those phone calls that helped me to realize that no matter what happened to me, there was an army of people out there all prepared to do whatever they could to ensure that my wife and children would make it through.

And so it is with the utmost sincerity that I say, THANK YOU. May your Christmas be merry and your New Year extraordinary.

Kyle, Brynn, Grace, Isaiah, Noah, and Bingo

Ervin Family Christmas Photo 2007

CHAPTER THIRTEEN
Rogue Waves

Brynn and Anthony were my central focus during these dark days, but they were not all that I had to be worried about. Beyond the tubes and monitors, beyond the NICU and the CVU, beyond the walls of Anaheim Regional Hospital, Grace, Isaiah, and Noah needed me. They felt the loss of their mother just as keenly as I felt the loss of my wife, and I could not orphan them to the situation. They needed their dad around to help them through it.

Like me, their roiling emotions would bubble over into tears and frustration, but where I punched holes in doors, my children expended their emotions in other ways.

In particular, I remember one night, gently scolding my oldest son, Isaiah, for breaking some rule or other only to have him completely fly off the handle. "I want my mom back! I hate you! I miss my mom!"

Taken aback by the verbal attack, I picked up my son and sat him down on the ottoman.

"Leave me alone!" he yelled at me and squirmed from my grasp. "Everybody's mean to me! You're mean to me! My mommy is sick! You're supposed to be nice to me!"

I was shocked, and frightened by the outburst. I think of Isaiah as my deep river. He feels very deeply, but like a deep river he is not easily moved. When he is upset, he will usually go off into his room and sulk. This explosion of inconsolable rage was very out of character for him.

"Buddy, I know this is hard for you. Mom is in the hospital and she will not be back for a very long time. I know you miss your momma." I began to choke up as I spoke. "I miss her, too. I miss her SO much. But there is nothing you or I can do about it. I know it makes you angry. It makes me angry, too. But that doesn't mean that we get to misbehave. We can't let Mommy being sick be an excuse to be naughty."

His blue eyes, like lasers, glowered at me from beneath his prominent dark brows. Tears dripped down his face over his five-year-old cheeks, which were bright red with the exertion of crying.

"Do you understand? Daddy's not going to let you get away with anything just 'cause Mommy's sick."

Finally, after a long moment, he nodded.

"Before Mommy was sick, did you get what you wanted if you cried?"

He shook his head.

"It's the same now. Do you understand?"

He glowered at me again, stubbornly unwilling to give way.

"Do you understand?"

He nodded.

"Good. Can I get a hug?"

He hugged me and melted into my arms and began to cry again, wetting my shoulder with his tears. I held his little sobbing body in my arms and began to cry, too, and together we let Fear out through our tears.

This must have been a bit strange for Isaiah because crying does not happen very often in our household. I simply do not allow it unless there is good reason. My admonishment for my children, when I feel they are crying for no good reason, is: "Put your tears away." It is my way of teaching them that there are things in life

121

that are worth crying over, and there are things that are not. You don't get the candy you want—"Put your tears away." A scuffed knee—"Put your tears away and walk it off." Fall off your scooter face first onto the concrete—"Yeah, okay you can cry for that one." Mom in a coma—"Yeah, you can cry for that one, too."

In fact, while Brynn was in the hospital, crying became a family affair just about every night at bedtime. We gathered on the bed as a family, snuggled up together, cried and comforted each other as we all tried to get to sleep.

The first night we tried this, I had them all pray for their mother, which turned out to be a mistake. It simply brought to their minds that which they were trying to forget, *had* to forget, in order to sleep. We would pray for her in the mornings from then on, when we would have the business of the day to get in the way of the dark thoughts those prayers would bring.

Besides gathering with all three kids at bedtime, I tried other things in an effort to give them the emotional support they needed to deal with their mother's situation. This is how I came up with "Daddy Time." Daddy Time was a chunk of time in which each one of them got me to themselves for a short while, and we did something special like go to a movie or just go to the park. Though Daddy Time started out as a conscious effort on my part to ensure that all of my children were getting the emotional support they needed, it ended up helping me as much or more than it did them. Caught in the hurricane-force wind, my three oldest children became my rudder and my ballast, keeping me moving in a direction and keeping me from capsizing emotionally and physically.

Despite the counterbalancing effect of my children, I was still sailing through treacherous waters. It was as though I were rounding Cape Horn, praying for good weather, but being met by fierce winds and fiercer waves, rogue waves that would crash over my bow, flooding me, trying to pull me under.

Why me? An inevitable question. *Why am I at the center of this? Why are you trying to drown me by taking from me my lover, my best friend, my teammate? What did I do that was* **SO** *wrong that you would take her from me? I know how she smells, how she breathes, how she raises her eyebrow when she hears something that just doesn't make sense. Why would you take her? Why would you leave in her place this profound emptiness that I fall into without warning?*

These rogue waves of emptiness caught me unawares at the strangest moments. I think this is because it was not the differences in my life that caught me off guard. It was not the trips to the hospital, or the sight of IV bags or feeding tubes. Those things, I was prepared for. Before walking into the hospital, I would put my mental life vest on to protect me from the trauma such sights might induce.

What got to me were the similarities to my old life. It was the daily, the mundane, the routine that came out of nowhere, washed up on my deck, knocked me off my feet and threatened to pull me out to sea. Old clothes, old songs, the smell of hair conditioner, these were the things that surprised me at the helm, forcing me to turn into them, praying I would have the speed to make it over them before they crashed over me and dragged me to the bottom.

One night, after I had put the kids to bed, I jumped in the shower to wash away the day. I stood there, tilting my head back slightly and let the hot water beat down on my chest. The water felt good and comforting on my skin. It streamed down my body, then down the drain, taking with it the accumulated tension of the day. I turned around to let the water beat down on my back and saw there, in the corner shampoo basket, my wife's shampoo and conditioner.

I suddenly found myself in Target two years prior. I was holding bottles of shampoo and conditioner in my hands. "Oh my God! This is what you spend on this stuff? This is insane!"

"It's what works best."

"What do you mean?"

"It doesn't wash the color out and keeps my hair soft. Anyway, I'm worth it, aren't I?"

I rolled my eyes at her.

"You want your wife to be pretty? Don't you?" She raised her eyebrows, tilting her head coquettishly.

"I'm not sure." I smiled. "At these prices I might be okay with an ugly wife." I tossed the bottles into our cart.

Back in the shower, the memory washed over me in an instant and, just like that, I had fallen into the emptiness again. I leaned against the cold tile of the shower and sobbed, letting all the emotion, every feeling of unfairness and injustice and anger that had built up inside me, pour out into the bath and down the drain. *Why me? This isn't fair. What did I do to deserve this?*

Then my mother's and father's voices entered my head, *Whoever told you that life was fair?* This was something I often heard as a child whenever I uttered, "It's not fair!"

The admonition always stung. I wanted life to be fair. I guess I actually still do. Yet, as I learned then and now know, they were right. Life isn't fair, and sometimes it just downright sucks.

I questioned whether God had made a trade with me, giving me my son and taking my wife. And then, I thought, *No, God would not make that trade, would he?* Then my mind tumbled into an answer. *What do I know about what God would do? Maybe I am being punished or taught a lesson about life's value.*

Because, truth be told, as much as it kills me to say it, I was ready for Anthony to die; I was as ready as a father can be. He was supposed to die. His tiny body was supposed to succumb to the stresses of life in utero. And, though I did not realize I was even doing it, I had spent six months preparing for that loss.

There is no rule book, no instruction manual to help a father prepare for such a thing. So I ended up letting my mind do what it would to protect me. And, though I love all my children beyond measure, I detached myself and distanced myself emotionally from the child that might never see the light of day.

If he lives, I will get to know him then. I will fall in love with him later. I will trust in his smile and his laugh to bring him into my heart. But if he dies, I must be able to focus on the living. I cannot get drawn too far into grief. I must be able to put him into the ground and move forward. Life is relentless. Life will not wait for me to get over it. My wife will be depending on me. My other children will be depending on me. Life will not stop for me to grieve so I must prepare myself to move on, and quickly.

Life is not only relentless. It is full of surprises. For six months, I prepared for one horrible possibility only to be completely blindsided by a totally different horror.

Were you trying to teach me something, God? 'Cause, screw you, if this is the way you teach. And I was angry with God again. And in the very next breath, I was bargaining with him. *I promise I will be a better person. You name it, I will do it. Just save my wife, please! Just bring her back to me!*

I was desperate, because the pulmonary embolism did not just take my wife from me. It took the one person that made me a whole and complete being. Without her, I was lost, I was broken, I was less than I was.

*Why am I being drowned? Why do you send these waves at **me**?*

Fear took advantage. He burrowed deep into my mind and reminded me of all the things I counted on Brynn for: her gentleness, her patience, her strength, and quite frankly her organization. I am many things, but detail-oriented is not one of them.

Brynn was the one who remembered to feed the children when lunchtime rolled around, and to change their diapers frequently to avoid diaper rash. She was the one who gave them their antibiotics three times a day for ten days, and the one who made sure they brushed their teeth and got their vitamins.

I struggled to keep my head above water. Fear, now my constant companion, struggled to bring me under. He whispered in my ear, *You are no good without her. You cannot care for your children by yourself, especially that little one. He will need way more than you can provide.*

When he began to overwhelm me with these whispers and I began to gag on the salty water, I sometimes just left the hospital and went to the local coffee shop, where I was as anonymous as the woman standing in line in front of me. I could pretend that life was normal for fifteen minutes or maybe a half hour. It was like finding a floating piece of debris. I could hold on to it and catch a breath. Other times, though, I sought a much stranger flotation device—the neonatal intensive care unit.

I know seeking sanctuary in the NICU seems insane. It actually is insane. NICUs are not normally places where parents can go to "get away." They are usually places where parents go to face Fear eye to eye. In the NICU, there is no escaping the facts. Your child's fight for life is written in real time, right in front of you; a constant story as told by a heart rate monitor, oxygen saturation sensor, thermometer, and respiration counter.

For me, it was different though. There was something

about being in that relatively small space, behind that locked door, that helped me to feel somewhat safe from what lie on the other side, as if what lie opposite the door was another life that had nothing to do with me.

I think it had something to do with the fact that Anthony was doing so well compared to Brynn. Despite his size and his challenges, I could usually expect some good news in the NICU. Though, looking back, I know that my own willing ignorance of his condition sometimes blinded me to the risks he faced.

A few days into the ordeal, I crossed the threshold of the NICU, closed the door behind me, and walked over to Anthony's incubator. The nurses had moved his IV from his hand to a vein on his head. The positioning looked strange but made sense. Finding a vein on such a small body has got to be difficult.

The nurse filled me in on his condition. "He's doing pretty well, but we've had to stop feeding him. He hasn't been digesting all the formula between feedings."

I don't think I said anything in response to this, so she went on to explain, "When they're this small, they can have problems with their digestive tract. So we're going to have to start over again with just a little bit of formula and slowly get him back up to where he was."

I can't tell you if it was the rather nonchalant way that she explained it, or whether it was because Brynn was facing, what seemed to me, much greater difficulties; but the fact that they had stopped feeding Anthony barely registered on my "oh crap" meter. I did not wonder or interrogate her as I might have only a few days prior. I just allowed her confident tone of voice convince me that this was par for the course.

"Oh. Okay," I replied to the news. "Can I hold him?"

"Of course."

It turns out, what they were probably worried about

is a condition called necrotizing enterocolitis, a potentially fatal condition. Fortunately, I remained blissfully unaware of this at the time. If I had known, I don't think the NICU would have been the refuge I so needed.

Anthony did get over his little digestive tract problem and began growing at a ferocious rate. He put on ounces per day. As he continued to improve, the NICU became more and more of a refuge for me. I relished my time there.

When I was not able to be there, I had the added blessing of knowing that I did not need to worry about him. He had the world's greatest babysitters looking after him—the NICU nurses. They fed him, changed him, kept him warm, and held him when we could not. It was incredibly comforting to know that he was being looked after by them twenty-four hours a day, seven days a week. It was one less thing I had to stress about.

Beyond the nurses, his grandparents and his aunt Katie did a great deal to relieve me of my responsibility to him. They learned how to feed him and burp him and make the regular trips, every four hours, to the NICU to make sure that was done.

This task was a great deal harder than it sounds. He was so small that it was imperative that he finish his bottle within twenty minutes. Otherwise he was expending too much energy to eat. The twenty-minute rule was, in fact, a prerequisite to him leaving the NICU.

Unfortunately, he had a nasty habit of quitting about halfway through. Katie and the grandparents had to learn tricks like pressing the nipple against the roof of his mouth, or rotating it, or actually pressing on his chin a little bit just to get him to eat. If he did not finish the bottle in time, he would be put back onto the feeding tube and fed that way.

Burping him was worse. This task seemed to be an exercise in sadism. The nurse who showed me how to burp him flipped him around like he was a toy doll, held his tummy against the heel of her hand, and banged on his back as though he were a particularly stubborn bottle of ketchup.

"You can't be shy about it," she told me. "You've got to knock him pretty good."

We had to knock him so hard to get a burp out that the grandmothers and Katie had a hard time getting it done. They just wouldn't hit him hard enough.

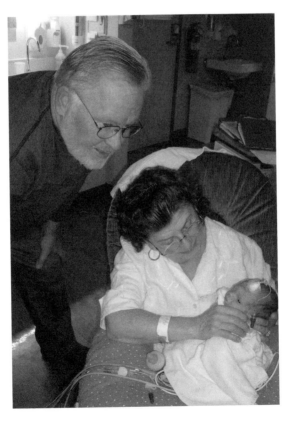

Grammies and Bubba Ervin and Anthony

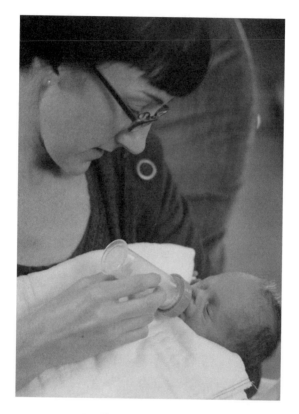

Auntie Katie with Anthony

Thanks to my incredible family and the amazing nurses, while Anthony was in the NICU, I could almost forget about him. It was weeks before I would feed him, and months before I changed his diaper.

In that strange way the world works—because I did not *have* to be in the NICU, it became a place I enjoyed. While I was there, I took the time to do for him what none of the others could do. They could not be his father. So, when I needed a break from Brynn's bedside, I escaped there for "skin to skin" time with my son.

I took off my shirt and donned the hospital gown.

Then I sat in a chair. Hopefully it was the comfortable rocking chair, but sometimes the rocker was taken by another parent, usually a mother nursing her child. If the rocker was taken, I sat in a less comfortable straight-back chair. One of the nurses would take him from the incubator, disconnecting all of the leads and tubes, and hand him to me. The tangle of cables and tubes dangled from his tiny body. I put him on my chest and rocked him.

As I rocked him, I talked to him. "I'm sorry my chest is so hairy." Looking down, I saw his wrinkled little face mashed up against the hair of my chest. Together we looked like something from a Dian Fossey documentary on gorillas.

"That doesn't look very comfortable," I said to him. "Your momma would be doing this right now if she could, but she's sick and we need to pray for her. Can you say a prayer for your momma... you were just there," I said, my voice cracking a bit with the raw emotion of the moment. "You still speak the language. Tell God you need your momma."

I imagined him reaching back, behind his sleeping eyes, to the place he had just come from, speaking the language we are all born with but forget with time, and asking God to save his momma. It brought me some peace of mind to imagine that.

Though the NICU became a refuge for me, I have to admit it was definitely a conditional refuge. I was still worried about the tiny baby I could hold in one out-stretched hand. The same machines that buzzed and beeped alarms at Brynn's bedside buzzed and beeped at Anthony's, causing the same sense of panic in me that they did downstairs.

Fortunately, as Anthony got stronger, and the nurses became more confident in his health, they took pity on me and turned them off while I held him. No, it was not a huge respite. I was still hanging on to a piece of debris and floating in an infinite ocean, but it was something—enjoying a few peaceful moments, finally bonding with the son I thought would die, recharging my batteries for a few more hours.

Once recharged, and knowing that he was in great hands, I went back downstairs to be with Brynn, wary of the waves that could crash over me at any moment.

Christmas Letter, 2008

Hello again, all, and welcome to another installation of the Ervin Family Year-end Letter. Sorry it's so late but for my excuse please see Appendix One (Trip to Indianapolis).

For new initiates to this yearly family history, please know that this is generally a PG-13 document. Daddy doesn't hold much back (though I swore to Brynn that I wouldn't tell everybody that we got caught "in the act" for the first time by a child we thought was in deep REM). Sorry, honey, that's just too funny to leave out. Oh look, sweetness, your cheeks are turning red.

Anyway, that particular familial hiccup is a perfect segue into a small truth that I've discovered over six years of parenting—"normal" is a remarkably relative term. And one's definition of "normal" changes drastically when kids come into the picture. I give you some examples to prove my point:

Before Children: Poop on your hands was likely to induce vomiting.

After Children: Eh, nothing a little soap won't take care of.

Before Children: Breasts were sexy.

After Children: Breasts are cheap portable

snack dispensers.

Before Children: Toilets were the only place for poop.

After Children: You have a "best practice" for removing turds from the tub.

Before Children: Making love was a marathon event.

After Children: Making love is a world record setting Olympic sprint. As is evident by our getting caught, I've got some work to do to get my time down. But I've purchased a stopwatch.

Yep, folks, the definition of "normal" really takes a beating when that first kid is born. Now, having shared this small truth of human existence for your enlightenment, I will move on to filling you in on the Ervin Family 2008.

It seems to be fitting to start with Isaiah, again, as the vast majority of gray hairs from 2008 can be directly attributed to him. To start with, he's definitely inherited his dad's propensity for head injuries. Yes, the ER doctor knows him by sight now (not an exaggeration). This propensity has had an oddly positive impact, however, as it was one of those head injuries that led to a CT scan of his head. This scan, in turn, led to the discovery of a rather large arachnoid cyst in his brain.

"WHAT THE F#@% IS THAT!!!???" you ask. Yep that was my first reaction too. Fortunately (after weeks of being sick to my stomach with worry for my son and multiple visits to neurologists and neurosurgeons), I can tell you, it's nothing much to worry about for now. It's something that develops in utero, and most people who have them go their whole lives not knowing that they are there.

However, there is a very small chance that

it could grow and begin to put pressure on the brain in which case it would require surgery. So, we are on the "wait and see" treatment plan in which he goes in every year for an MRI, and we "wait and see" whether it has grown at all.

He's been a champ through it all, though. He makes his daddy proud. Now if I can just get him to accept the fact that Noah will be with us for a while. He adores his sister, but would be perfectly happy, I think, if the stork came back for his little brother.

As for that little brother, Noah is doing well. He talks quite a bit now and is very animated. The only problem is he doesn't seem to be speaking any recognizable human language. My theory: I think he's speaking in tongues. I mean, doesn't it make perfect sense that God would want to speak through a child of mine? I think so.

Beyond his supernatural language abilities, he has acquired a new nickname. I've started to call him "Wedge." No, this is not an allusion to, Wedge Antilles, the only secondary character to be in all three of the original *Star Wars* movies. If you know what I'm talking about here you are a total geek!—Josh—Chris.

Anyway, he gets the nickname because he will, upon seeing dad hugging mom, wedge himself between us and push us apart. And, so you say, "Just let the kid fall asleep." Except that he has an uncanny ability to wake himself as soon as dad even imagines he might get some. Another nickname I was kicking around was WBC or "walking birth control," but it doesn't quite roll off the tongue as nicely as Wedge.

And then there's Grace. I love my little girl but, man, do I have to be careful around her.

She is far more aware of her surroundings then her parents might like. She listens to and absorbs everything!

Example: We were out to dinner for my birthday, and Brynn and I were discussing who would be the designated driver. Grace chimes in out of the blue, "It's Daddy's birthday, so it's his turn to get drunk." She's six years old, people. There goes my Parent of the Year Award.

Not only is she hyper-aware of everything we say and do, but her abilities to manipulate us improve with every passing year. Now, part of this is my fault, as I thought I should teach her about negotiation from an early age—BAD IDEA!!!

She's a better negotiator at six than I was at twenty-six. The other day she wanted a juice box (which we limit, due to the sugar), so she says, "Daddy, can I have a piece of candy, or a juice box?" She didn't even give me a chance to say no, only to say yes to one of two options. I am in SO MUCH TROUBLE!

As if the three kids and a dog weren't enough, we decided to add a cat to the family this year. This addition actually had a very practical purpose. You see, there was a rather large contingent of field mice who were using my garage as a staging area for their eventual attempt at world domination. Crookshanks was brought in last spring to deal with them. And so far he has done a fine job. He has already delivered to our porch numerous small animal body parts.

There are some downsides to having a cat in the house. The major one is that we've discovered that our dog, Bingo, has a rather disgusting addiction to cat crap. Unbeknownst to us, cat crap is like doggy crack cocaine. We've considered an intervention, but his addiction has a rather significant benefit for us in that we don't have to clean the litter box nearly as often. So, the intervention may have to wait.

As for me, I'm doing well. I didn't lose my wallet once this year!!!—Well, at least not for more than a day. I'm not even Catholic, but I've definitely developed an affinity for St. Anthony (patron saint of lost things). He's a great saint to know if you happen to have a *slight* case of ADD.

Not only do I have the same wallet but I have the same job, too! The folks at Vironex seem to like me well enough and I like them, too. There are probably two people in the whole office who don't have some level of ADD; man, you should hear some of our conversations. But it's a great group of people to work with and it's a heck of a lot of fun working for a company that's on the cutting edge of the industry.

I've also been cancer-free for over a year, which is cool. I've been diagnosed with type-2 diabetes, which is not cool. But I'm doing my best to eat better and get more exercise.

I still can't seem to keep up with all the stuff that needs doing around my house. I did finally get my workbench built; it's only been seven years. The front bathroom is still a disaster. The laminate flooring I installed is warping in the kitchen where a hidden drain backed up. And the water heater took a dump the day before we were set to leave on vacation. Oh, and did I mention that the microwave also took a crap? And because it's an over-counter with a fan, it's going to cost roughly twice as much as a normal microwave. Yep, I'm convinced that my house is out to get me.

The backyard is the one thing that is shaping up due to the simple fact that we have an absolutely monstrous play structure back there. Astronauts look down into my backyard and say, "Damn, I wish I had a play structure like that!"

The structure is courtesy of Grammies and Bubba Ervin who bought it from their neighbor, took it apart, drove it down here, refinished <u>every</u> piece and then spent a month putting it back together. Yes, did you catch that??? A MONTH.

I had to live with my parents again for a whole month. I love my mom and pops but it was like being back in high school, minus the binge drinking on the weekends.

It was totally worth it, though. For one, they do really good work. It was one of those occasions where having a meticulous father, and a mother who knows her way around carpentry tools, was extremely beneficial.

Beyond that, the play structure has made my life a zillion times easier. I now have zero qualms about kicking my kids outside so mom and dad can have some quiet time. THANKS, Grammies and Bubba!

As for Brynn, she is doing fairly well. She's now teaching third grade. Her principal thought she would be a good fit for third because of the "rigor" she brings to her classroom (Okay, sorry to digress, but how's that for total irony. Not only did I marry a teacher, but I married the "tough" teacher.) Anyway, she is totally excited and happy with the switch, but she is still having trouble getting used to the rampant nose-picking that goes on in that grade level.

Beyond trading grades, she will also be taking on a student teacher in the New Year which will bring new challenges. But I'm so incredibly proud of her.

Her health has taken a beating this year, though. She took a hard spill on the steps of my parent's vineyard, bruising her tailbone badly and tearing her rotator cuff. She had an MRI of the shoulder done and was found to have something called Chiari malformation in her brain.

"WHAT THE F#@% IS THAT!!!???" you ask. Yep, that was my first reaction, too. Fortunately, like Isaiah, this turns out to be a condition that is nothing much to worry about—right now. There is the potential for some rather serious problems and she is not allowed to ride roller coasters anymore but as of right now she's good and we're incredibly thankful for that (Who am I kidding? **I'M** incredibly thankful for that. I'd be up to my eyes in crap without her)

I am in the market for a family neurosurgeon though. So if any of you know somebody who's really good and willing to work cheap, let me know.

As for the two of us, we've been married now for the infamous seven years, and the only "itch" I get is to get rid of the kids for an hour so that I can get some mommy time. It's difficult to explain how my love for her grows year after year. But what I think it amounts to is that when everything is breaking, she calms me and she loves me. When the frustration of life is so intense that all I want to do is destroy things, she pulls me out of it, reminds me that life's not meant to be perfect, reminds me of how lucky I am—even with a kitchen that is falling apart, a broken water heater and a disastrous front bathroom. Not only all of that, but she doesn't get mad at me when I lose things—not even when I lose my wallet.

Sooooo, it's been another doozy of a year for the Ervins. And we wouldn't have it any other way—well, of course we would, if we had a choice—but we don't, so we take *it* as it comes, and deal the best way that we know how. And now we enter another year, ready for whatever it has in store for us. We're ready because we have each other, but more importantly, we're ready because we're truly blessed to have all of you. Thank you, each and every one of you, for being there for us. We love you.

Happy New Year
Kyle, Brynn, Grace, Isaiah, Noah, Bingo, and Crookshanks

Appendix One—The Trip to Indianapolis

The whole reason I waited to write this year's "Year-end Letter" is that I knew our family would be making a trip to Indianapolis, for the first time, to visit Auntie Alisa for Christmas. And I was certain that such a trip, with three small children, would provide a bounty of anecdotes that might fit well into the letter. Little did I know just how prescient I was. The fact of the matter is that when I included the trip in the letter, it was about seven pages. And even *I* know that is a lot of Ervinness to ask anybody to slog through. So, in an effort to break things up for you, my readers, I've simply added the trip as an appendix to the letter... read it if you like, or burn it in the fireplace. Well, actually you should probably recycle it, unless you're one of those global warming doubters. Anyway, here's how it went down...

The trip began on December 20 as the five of

us made our way to John Wayne Airport. Now, because United Airlines (who will heretofore be referred to as "The Bastards" for reasons that will become apparent) charge for each checked bag, Brynn and I crammed everything for our trip, including clothes, diapers, Christmas presents, a DVD player, etc., into two checked bags and five small carry-ons, every single one of which was ready to burst upon the slightest provocation. It was quite a feat of packing prowess, I must say. However, upon checking in (with a very long line of people also waiting to check in), we learned that our largest check-on bag was nine pounds overweight. To send it at that weight was going to cost $125. So, right there on the airport floor, with the delicacy of a bomb disposal expert, I carefully unzipped the bag. I could feel my face redden as the contents exploded upon the linoleum.

I began searching for the densest items and frantically handed them to Brynn so that she could, hopefully, find a place for them in one of the other bags. In the meantime, Noah had decided that this was a good time to go exploring. So off he went, into the line of people and plopped down on his back in the middle of the floor. Brynn and I looked over, both of our hands filled with the contents of our luggage, to see him laying there, looking up at people with a huge smile on his face as if it were the most natural thing in the world. My wife's cheeks were a shade of red not normally found in nature.

We did manage to get our bag down to about fifty-one pounds before the guy behind the counter took pity on us and let us check it. From there, we did a rather good job of getting to the gate with only minor embarrassment as we delayed the security line. After all that rushing, however, we learned that our flight was delayed. So we got the kids some McDonald's (because what else is there to eat in airports?) and did our best to entertain the three of them while we waited.

Once in the air, we pulled out our super secret weapon—Children's Benadryl—and breathed a sigh of relief as our three children curled up and drifted off into blissful, albeit antihistamine-induced, sleep. Now, please understand that we are not in the habit of drugging our children to sleep, but I am absolutely unapologetic about it. If you were there, you'd understand.

After a five-hour flight, we landed amidst snow flurries in Chicago and made it to our connecting gate without much fanfare only to find that our connecting flight would also be delayed— THREE HOURS! So we got the kids some more McDonald's and did our best to entertain the three of them while we waited. Luckily, Chicago O'Hare has those moving walkways and those kept us entertained for at least ninety minutes.

We finally arrived in Indianapolis at 2:00 a.m. their time to find that Noah's car seat did not get on the plane with us. After getting a loaner car seat, we made it to my sister's house around 4:00 a.m. (which really isn't so bad, because we're still on Cali time so it's really only 1:00 a.m. Oh wait, that's still frickin' late.)

Now, my father is an intelligent man. I mean he has a master's degree in chemistry, for God's sake. So why he thought it might be a good idea to show his grandchildren the electric train at 4:00 a.m. is way beyond me. I'm going to chalk that one up to grandparental exuberance. But we did finally manage to get all three kids to sleep somewhere near sunrise.

Our first day in Indianapolis was relatively un-eventful. We all woke up very late and basically spent the day convalescing. The children discovered the Disney Channel (we don't have TV at home) and were quick to pick up the art of operating the DVR. We did try to go for a walk, and Grace, Isaiah, and I made it around the block before the minus twenty-two wind chill sent us home. Mommy didn't even make it off the driveway, and Noah increased his vocabulary by forty percent, saying, "So cold! So cold!," over and over again.

Day two, we took some family photos, and did some shopping. But the real excitement was the horse-drawn carriage ride through downtown Indianapolis. It was cold enough to freeze snot (I know this because my snot froze in my mustache) and the eight of us crammed into a carriage meant to hold four. Poor Domino (the horse pulling the carriage) had his work cut out for him.

We were having the sort of delirious fun that families have when they're stuffed tightly into the back of horse-drawn carriages in sub-freezing temperatures. We were piled high in blankets, singing Christmas carols, and watching other horse-drawn carriages pass us with ease when our digital camera slipped off Grammies' wrist and fell into the middle of the street. Domino skidded to a halt and I jumped out into the middle of the road to get it. But I was only fast enough to see it be crushed by a car—twice.

It was that night, or rather very early the next

morning, that Gracie, her tummy upset from ingesting the copious amounts of unhealthy food that come with being on vacation, puked all over the bed—and in mom's hair.

Luckily, we had a washing machine at my sister's place right? WRONG.

While mom's washing the puke sheets, Isaiah discovered that the basement toilet was not flushing. Bubba went downstairs to find out what was going on only to find the laundry room flooded with four feet of bubbles. No kidding, people, it was like that episode of *The Brady Bunch* when Bobby floods the washroom with suds.

It turned out there was something wrong with the basement plumbing and eight people now had to share one bathroom for the next five days. Furthermore, the washing machine was out of commission, and we'd only brought five days worth of clothes in order to save on luggage.

Fortunately, Gracie felt better after puking, and we all piled into the rental van for a trip to some outlying areas. **Un**fortunately, that was the day a horrible ice storm hit. Essentially, the greater Indianapolis area became a giant skating rink for automobiles. I'll admit, it's kinda fun to watch when you're in California. But being in it kinda stinks. Our plans smashed for that day, we headed back to sis' house for some more Disney Channel and, of course, a good amount of playing Superman from the couch to the mattress on the floor.

WE'RE NOT EVEN HALFWAY THROUGH THE TRIP, PEOPLE!

The next day was Christmas Eve. My sis, being the sweetheart that she is, found a nice Catholic Church so my wife and kids wouldn't miss Mass. Bubba stayed home to deal with the plumber. He was also tasked by Grammies to remove the roast from the oven.

While we were at Mass, Bubba did all number of things. He cleaned up the basement, fixed the fridge door handle, and dealt with the plumber (he's always been a bit hyperkinetic that way). He didn't, however, remove the roast from the oven.

Upon learning that the roast was now one step removed from charcoal, Grammies let loose on Bubba with both barrels; this is the reason there is a twenty-four-hour waiting period for handgun purchases. It actually only took her about twenty minutes to cool down, but we were all afraid for his life for a minute there.

Luckily, sis had a few packets of mushroom gravy, and we were able to partially recover Christmas Eve dinner.

Christmas day was very nice. It was one of those crisp winter days when the sun is shining but the cold refuses to give up its hold on the land. We all sat around the tree and opened presents and drank lots and lots of coffee. The kids and I went for a run around the block, and they enjoyed "skating" on the icy puddles we found.

Christmas dinner was another matter however. Grammies was in the midst of preparing beef stroganoff when one of my sister's dogs got a hold of the plate with the sautéed mushrooms and shattered it on the kitchen floor (I gotta say here that Grammies gave the dog a lot more leeway that she did Bubba the night before).

Being Christmas in Indiana, there was no hope of finding replacement mushrooms, so we ended up with Kraft Mac n Cheese and hamburgers.

The day after Christmas, I was able to do a load of laundry at the Laundromat and buy a duffle bag to cram all the gifts in for the trip home. Grammies was finally able to complete a meal—and the beef stroganoff was well worth the wait.

On Saturday, we loaded up the van and set off for Indianapolis airport. By this point we're pros at mobilizing our family of five through the airport and make it to our gate without much fanfare—where our flight is delayed for over an hour because United, (Oh, that's right) The Bastards, didn't have a flight crew. I began to get worried about making our connecting flight (even though we had a three-hour layover), so I called The Bastards to see about other possible flights to Orange County. After being stuck on an automated phone service for half an hour, I finally got to talk to a nice chap somewhere in India. The earliest flight they could find to anywhere near Orange County was Tuesday—THREE DAYS LATER!

Fortunately, our plane began to board with a takeoff time that would get us to Chicago with enough time to make our flight. **Un**fortunately, it then sat on the tarmac for two more hours. We ended up missing our connection in Chicago by ten minutes.

So, at this point, we're stuck in Chicago for three days with six diapers, the clothes on our backs, and all the Christmas toys you could ask for.

Resigned to our fate, we got the kids some

McDonald's and I got in the United Customer Service (heretofore to be known as the United Customer "Screw You" Line).

While in line we learn that The Bastards do not provide rooms for people stuck due to "weather related" issues. This despite the fact that The Bastards' own pilot said the weather was not really that bad in Chicago, and it was a lack of flight crew that led to the initial delay. Whatever. They gave us a coupon for a reduced rate at a local hotel and told Brynn that the courtesy shuttle leaves every half hour. By this time it's about 10:00 p.m. and we mobilize our kids, once again, for a mile-long trek to the shuttle area.

We are waiting for the Holiday Inn Select shuttle. We wait for about thirty minutes and see shuttles for every derivation of Holiday Inn that exists except for The Holiday Inn Select. After forty-five minutes, I call the hotel to find out what's going on only to learn that the shuttle is by request after 10:00 p.m. We're closing in on eleven o'clock and I'm more than a little pissed off. We wait another thirty to forty minutes before the shuttle finally arrives. However, in the time we've been waiting, some sixty people have arrived, all waiting for the same shuttle. They all make a mad dash for the shuttle door while we're standing there trying to mobilize.

At this point, I'm bordering on homicidal and barge my way to the van door. I tell the shuttle driver that my family and I are getting on the shuttle come hell or high water and let him know with my best thousand-mile stare that I'm willing to go to blows with anybody who thinks that's not going to happen. I shout to Brynn to bring the kids through the mob that has gathered outside the door. But she is quicker to see the futility of my bluster and probably doesn't want me getting arrested, so she calls me off.

Utterly defeated, we walked across the street to the Airport Hilton (A hotel I know I can't afford) and pulled out the American Express to the tune of 200 dollars a night. We get into our room around midnight, but Brynn and I are so wound up we can't fall asleep until about 2:00 a.m.

We struggled through the next three days, stuck in Chicago with no clothes, in a hotel we couldn't afford, and tried to make the best of it. We swam in the very cold pool. The kids watched even more Disney Channel. We washed clothes in the bathroom sink (not extraordinarily effective by the way). We went to the Sears Tower (not worth the money or the wait). And we tried with all our might to find a pizza place.

You would think downtown Chicago would be bubbling over with pizza joints—not the case. We searched for hours before finding a nice little place that didn't even serve Chicago-style pizza! It was very good pizza, but not Chicago style. And finally (I'm not proud to admit this), I dragged my family to the seediest liquor store I've ever been to, because it was the only place I could find that sold alcohol. But come on! After all that, I NEEDED a drink.

I do have to say that we did run into many angels along the way. One gentleman helped us with the luggage when we were trying to get to the shuttle, and probably missed it himself for his kindness. One woman found us some diapers, and another lent Brynn her cell phone charger. And there was the hotel coupon lady who got us a reduced rate at the Hilton for the last two nights (though, still more than we could afford).

But we ran into some real stinkers, too—most of them worked for United. It was as if the fact that there were "weather conditions" gave them carte blanche to treat us with disdain. When we finally did get our flight, they put the five of us in three separate boarding groups. With three kids, how the hell is that supposed to work? When I gave the lady collecting the boarding passes all five at the same time she had the nerve to give me the stink eye. Brynn tried to be nice and explain that boarding the five of us at separate times wasn't going to work, and I had to tell her to stop trying to be nice to these people 'cause they didn't deserve it.

After all that, Nana and Poppi Holderness were able to come and pick us up at LAX (I forgot to mention that we weren't able to fly back into John Wayne) and Poppi took me to John Wayne to retrieve the luggage and the car, to the tune of 148 dollars in long-term parking fees.

The trip was, of course, not a total bust. We got to spend Christmas with my family at my sister's new place. We got to see a part of the world we had never seen before, even parts of it we weren't intending to see. And we learned some very valuable lessons...

1) When traveling with three kids at Christmas, pay the extra fifteen dollars for an extra bag.
2) NEVER fly through Chicago at Christmastime.
3) NEVER again fly on United. I found the below on Wikipedia and totally understand why:

"May 2008, the American Customer Satisfaction Index scored United Airlines second-last among

US-based airlines in customer satisfaction with a 21% decrease since the study began in 1994 and an 11% decrease over the previous year."

4) The movie *Supersize Me* was not B.S. Eating that much McDonald's really does make you ill. At the very least, it binds you up something fierce.
5) Chicago-style pizza is easier to find in California than in Chicago.
6) Minibar drinks are nine dollars a pop at the Hilton.
7) Nine dollars a pop may be worth it if the only alternative is dragging three small kids and your terrified wife into a very scary liquor store.

So, lessons learned, and to be totally honest—a great story to get to tell. I've found that when the trip goes perfectly, there is generally very little to write about.

Happy New Year to All,
Kyle, Brynn, Grace, Isaiah, and Noah, Bingo, and Crookshanks

CHAPTER FOURTEEN

The Valley of the Shadow of Death

Psalm 23:4 *Even though I walk through the valley of the shadow of death, I fear no evil; for thou art with me; thy rod and thy staff, they comfort me.*

I'm no Bible thumper and I am not prone to quoting the Good Book, but I really like Psalm 23:4. I think I like it because I am a writer, and from a writer's perspective it is a very elegant sentence. It lets my own imagination do most of the work. It is a single sentence, but it conjures so much more.

In my mind I can see "the valley of the shadow of death." It is a dark, deep ravine, and there are sheer cliffs on either side. The valley floor is nothing but shadows and dampness. Stagnant pools reek of filth and decay. Dead thorny brambles clog the path and block my way. When I am in the valley, something evil lurks on the cliff side. Though I cannot see it, I know it is there and I know that it hunts me.

But then Psalm 23:4 goes on to tell me that God is there, too, and he is there to protect me. And I envision him, the embodiment of goodness and light, holding a staff ready to do battle with whatever darkness lurks there. In a single sentence, Psalm 23:4 can help me to overcome my very human tendency to run from things that frighten me, knowing that God has my back.

As it would turn out, "the valley of the shadow of death" was not the bramble clogged ravine that I had imagined. When I walked through it, it was a ten-by-twelve-foot hospital room and a NICU incubator, and I was not the one in jeopardy (well, at least not of dying).

When I walked through the "valley of the shadow of death," I did so trying to cuddle an impossibly tiny child, and holding my wife's hand, while a machine breathed for her and tubes fed them both. As I sat there, staring at IV pumps and vital signs, faith and doubt did battle. The truth is that doubt generally won out. There was so much bad news—so much working against her—faith really didn't stand a chance.

Now, when I speak of faith, I must be clear. During the entire ordeal, I never really lacked faith in God's existence. I still believed in God with every fiber of my being. I only lacked faith that he might intervene. I saw no reason why he might. I saw no reason why our family, so ordinary and simple, would be granted a miracle when so many other families in the world had to suffer the loss of loved ones. It simply wasn't logical.

Yet, despite my constant doubt, nearly every single day, I had something small to hold onto—something that helped to put my mind at ease so that I could sleep for the night. Though the overwhelming weight of the evidence suggested that my wife's death was inevitable, I always received some infinitesimal sign that, maybe, just maybe, God was with me, and maybe, just maybe, he was doing some work behind the scenes.

Perhaps I was just a self-deluded, grieving husband finding the positive where there was none. But I prefer to believe that God was telling me, in his own sweet way, "Be patient. Give me some time."

***

When they brought Brynn back to the CVU on the night of December 2, her pupils were, in the parlance of medical people, "eight and fixed." This means they were fully dilated (greater than eight millimeters in diameter) and not responsive to light.

One of the easiest ways for doctors and nurses to measure neurological function is by measuring the pupils' reaction to light. In neurological terms, eight and fixed is as bad as it gets. Fixed and dilated pupils indicate severe brain damage.

On December 3, I had heard through the grapevine that two doctors had seen different things in Brynn's pupils. One was still seeing her pupils as eight and fixed, whereas another noticed a very slight reaction when he shined his light in her eyes. On December 3, it was the opinion of the second doctor that I lived on for the day, and it was the thought of her slightly reactive pupils that helped me to sleep that night.

***

On Friday, December 4, I walked into the CVU waiting room and was greeted by the news that they were attempting to bring Brynn off of sedation. For almost two days, they had kept her in an induced coma while her body was in the artificial state of hypothermia. For two days, I waited. Finally, the previous evening, they had allowed her body to warm. It was now time to see how she would respond when they stopped giving her the sedative. There was a collection of people outside of her room. The nurses involved in her care, and even a nurse from Mission Hospital, had come in to offer support.

I walked into her room. "Hey, baby, can you open your eyes for me? Let me see your beautiful eyes."

Then, slowly, as if they weighed a thousand pounds, her eyelids opened. Her eyes were dazed and she looked off into nowhere. But she had opened her eyes. I was ecstatic. "That was all I needed, baby. That was all I needed."

Then her eyes rolled back and her legs began to twitch. I thought she might be shivering from the cold. I found out later that she was having a seizure. Neurologically speaking, this is a really bad sign. But at the time, I did not know that. At the time, all I saw was that she had OPENED HER EYES! And on Friday, December 4, that is what I held onto. The fact that she opened her eyes allowed me to sleep that night.

***

On Saturday, December 5, I arrived to the hospital a little later in the morning. The on-call neurologist had already been to see Brynn, and I had missed him. Whatever positive energy I had mustered that morning was completely obliterated by the fact that I missed him. I was in dire need of information, and the "not knowing" dragged me deeper into the Valley of Death.

This is when I learned the Murphy's Law of having a family member in critical condition—*no matter how many hours you spend at the bedside, you will always miss the doctor that you really need to talk to.*

Luckily, the nursing staff was kind enough to reach the neurologist by phone for me, and I spoke to him as he drove. He laid it on the line for me in the gentlest terms he could. "Your wife's EEG is showing signs of seizure. Basically there are three possible outcomes. One, she could die; two, things could stay the same (meaning persistent vegetative state); or three, miraculous recovery. I am honestly doubtful of the third option."

This news crushed me—again. A few words from a doctor, and I instantly fell deeper into a previously inconceivable black hole. To call what I felt "doubt" is disingenuous. A doctor, a trained neurologist, was telling me that, in all likelihood, my wife was going to die or remain a vegetable.

No, what I felt was not doubt. It was certainty. I was certain that my wife was never going to come out of her coma. The weight of this information, like the weight of the ocean, pushed in on me from all sides.

Brynn and I had discussed situations just like this, the way married couples often do. These conversations were usually spurred on by some news story about a family fighting over whether to keep a comatose relative alive or to "pull the plug." We always came down on the "pull the plug" side. We agreed that a life dependant on machines is no real life. It is a bastardization of life. Neither of us ever wanted to live in any sort of vegetative state. Neither of us ever wanted to live with tubes sticking out of us.

However, having had the discussion and then being faced with the reality of making such a decision were worlds apart. I knew what I was *supposed to do* if she did not progress from this point. But my wife HAD JUST OPENED HER EYES. How could I do this, after she had opened her eyes?

Fear worked on me the entire day as this possibility bounced around in my head. The thought of losing her tore at my heart. The responsibility of letting her go crushed me. *What will her family think of me? Her mother, her father, her sister, every other person that loves her as deeply as I do, if I have to "pull the plug."* Fear paralyzed me until I finally reached the conclusion that it was not a decision I could make.

As I walked alone through the hospital halls, Fear metamorphosed to anger, the raw emotion welled in my eyes. I yelled at God, "God, either take her or heal her, but none of this middle-of-the-road bullshit!"

Perhaps it's blasphemous to cuss at God, but at the

time I really did not care. I was mad.

Yet at some point that same day, something came to me, and whether it was my own imagination working feverishly to keep me in a positive mood or an angel whispering in my ear, I couldn't tell you. The truth of that really doesn't matter. What matters is it came to me. And what came to me was this—for this to be a miracle, an honest-to-God "turn water into wine" miracle—she would have to defy all of the odds and every prediction.

Suddenly, the fact that her condition was so incredibly dire, so impossible, was my rationalization for why she was going to make it. In the cynical world we live in, for God to get the credit, her recovery was going to have to be impossible.

When I look back on it, it was absolutely insane logic. In those dark days, however, that thought, that God was going to make a miracle, is what got me to sleep that night.

***

On Sunday, December 6, I was scheduled to meet with the neurologist I had spoken to the day before. I knew what time he would be doing rounds and made sure I was at the hospital at that time. I also knew he would be viewing some CT scans of Brynn's brain, and I needed to know what he saw.

By this time, I had realized that my mind's ability to process information had decreased significantly. Whenever I talked to a doctor or nurse, most of what they told me slid in one ear, slipped through the crevasses of my mind like gelatin down a waterslide, and then out the other ear. So, despite my lifelong abhorrence of asking my parents' advice, I asked my father to be with me when I met with the doctor.

I wanted my dad with me, in particular, because he has many attributes that make him valuable to have around when talking to doctors. First, as a trained chemist and scientist, I trusted him to bring at least some objectivity to what I was being told. Second, as the retired director of Technical Support for a company that makes blood glucose monitoring systems, he spent his career dealing with doctors on a collegial level and would never be intimidated by their title. But most important, from my point of view, was that with his background in the medical field and his analytical mind, he could take in the information being given, process it, and develop pertinent and intelligent questions.

My dad sat with me in the CVU waiting room, and the neurologist sat down across from us. He was a relatively young Asian man with intelligent eyes and a confident bearing. As he sat down, I tried to read his body language. I could read nothing.

He went on to explain that the nature of Brynn's trauma was severe and that her EEG or brain-wave scans were still showing signs of seizure. "However," he continued, "I did not see the damage I expected to in the CT scans."

He went on to explain that when the brain is without oxygen, the affected brain tissue essentially disintegrates into a pool of "goop." This damage shows up as a less dense area on the CT. "Now keep in mind that CTs are limited in what they can show." He went on, "And she is by no means out of the woods, but this gives us a small reason for hope."

Hope. *Thy rod and thy staff they comfort me.*

This was the first piece of evidence that might suggest even the possibility of some sort of recovery. And that was enough for me to sleep that night.

***

On Tuesday, December 8, I heard from yet another neurologist. He told me that Brynn's brain waves were still scattered and chaotic and that, on a scale of one to ten for neurological function, he had to give my wife a one or a two.

By this time, however, my own sense of how my wife was doing began to diverge from that of the doctors. It wasn't that I felt the doctors were mistaken in their analysis, but I did not feel that they were privy to all the data that I was.

They would come and examine Brynn for five or ten minutes every day, and they perused the data from her EEGs. Based on what they saw, I know why they were not optimistic. First off, her EEGs looked bad. I don't know how to read an EEG, but I do know how to read body language. And when the EEG tech looked at his screen, though he was not allowed to tell me anything, I could tell that what he saw was not good. The doctors would later confirm my suspicions.

Beyond the bad EEGs, there was also the fact that Brynn did not respond to *anything* while the doctors were in the room. She simply did not "perform." She did not respond to their voices. She did not respond to touch. She did not respond to the pain of being pinched hard in the eyebrow. Though she was comatose, I swear I could sense the stubborn Irish-Portuguese woman I had married, telling them in the only way she could, "*Screw you. If you're going to pinch me, I'm gonna just lie here. I can take the pain.*" Maybe she was being stubborn, maybe she was totally out of it; either way, she did not respond.

What I did not know is that there are many stages or levels of coma. The Glasgow Coma Scale is used as a rating system to give people an idea of what level or stage of coma a patient is in.

Glasgow Coma Scale		
Activity	**Level of Activity**	**Score**
Eye Opening	Spontaneously	4
	To Speech	3
	To Pain	2
	None	1
Verbal Response	Orientated	5
	Confused	4
	Inappropriate	3
	Incomprehensible	2
	None	1
Motor Response	Obeys Commands	6
	Localizes to Pain	5
	Withdraws from Pain	4
	Flexion to Pain	3
	Extension to Pain	2
	None	1
Maximum Score		15

Because of Brynn's lack of reaction to the doctors, she scored the absolute lowest possible on this scale. On top of all of this, Brynn had what is known as the Babinski sign present. This means that, when Brynn's foot was rubbed with a blunt instrument from her heal to her toes, instead of her toes curling down as they would in a healthy person, her toes curled up. The Babinski sign being present is indicative of damage to the central nervous system.

So, based on everything they were seeing, it is clear to me why they were so pessimistic.

I was at her bedside for hours, though. And between me and all of our family and friends, we were at her bedside pretty much the entire day. Throw in the things we heard from nurses, and we were privy to twenty-four-hours worth of data versus the doctors' five- to ten-minute examination.

We began to see things the doctors never did. The same day the neurologist had given her a one or a two, a technician came to her room to give her an ultrasound in search of more blood clots. As he ran the wand up her leg and onto her inner thigh, she jerked her leg up in apparent protest. That same day, when the nurses were washing her, she lifted up both arms as if to protest.

Where we most often saw a response from Brynn, though, was when the respiratory tech suctioned her. This process consisted of inserting a small vacuum tube into her intubation tube and down her larynx. Then, they would vacuum out all of the built-up phlegm. The process literally choked her and was extremely uncomfortable. Virtually every time I saw her have her chest suctioned, she opened her eyes wide in discomfort. When this happened I tried desperately to hold her attention for a moment. Sometimes I think I even succeeded.

I told the neurologists about these events, but they were, understandably, not inclined to give the observations of a grieving husband much credence. The likelihood that this woman, who had been through ninety-five minutes of cardiopulmonary arrest, was somehow starting to heal was tiny when compared to the possibility that a severely distraught husband was "seeing what he wanted to see."

I did see it, however. And because I saw it, hope still had a fighting chance against doubt. Naturally, my desire to see even the smallest signs that Brynn might recover became something of an obsession. Strangely enough, "hope," once it gets going, is powerfully addictive. Once I had it, I did not want to give it up for anything. Looking back, I can understand why doctors might ignore the observations of grieving family members. Hope is so powerfully addictive that many people will lie to themselves and others just to keep it.

For myself, I spent hours at her bedside wanting to see *something*—just *something*—that would get me through to the next day. It became such an obsession that I found myself one day hoping she would not do anything while I was gone—I didn't want to miss anything. The hope that I got from seeing her do something tiny far outweighed the hope I might find from being "told" she had done something.

As soon as I realized I was doing it, I realized how insanely selfish I was being. Yes, I wanted to be there to see every little thing, but ultimately the most important thing was for her to get better, whether I was there or not. That day, as I tore myself away from her bedside, I told her, "Don't be afraid to do something amazing without me." Then I walked upstairs to see my son.

***

When living our day-to-day lives and hearing stories of great tragedy, we may have moments of reflection, *How would I respond to such a situation? Would I be strong? Would I buckle under the weight of it? How would I react?* I know I used to do this. And when I did, I imagined myself in the situation and envisioned myself as a sturdy, unyielding fortress still capable of making cool, calculated decisions despite the chaos around me.

When the chaos did strike, the reality was much less flattering. Instead of the sturdy fortress I had envisioned myself as, I felt more like a palm tree in a hurricane, being whipped to and fro by insanely strong winds, bending and bending, hoping not to break.

"How are you doing?" people asked, concerned for my well-being. That was another question I had a hard time answering. I didn't want to lie and tell them "good" or "fine" or "all right," because it was an answer that was so obviously not true. But I also wanted to express that I wasn't "falling apart at the seams" either. I wasn't suicidal or having panic attacks or anything like that. It took me a few days, but I finally came up with a suitable answer, "I'm surviving."

As the winds of the hurricane blew, and I bent over under their force, I kept this thought in my head—*All you have to do is survive this. You do not need to be perfect, you do not need to be strong, just survive. Wake up every day and get out of bed, despite the wind that blows against you.*

So I fell back on a skill I had learned some fifteen years before as a recruit at Marine Corps Recruit Depot, San Diego. I broke the days up into small, survivable chunks. I woke up every morning, read my Facebook page, and cried as I read every single heartfelt post from family and friends. Those posts were akin to mail call at boot camp for me. I took in and relished every word, every thought, every prayer. They gave me the fortitude to make it through the morning.

After reading the posts, I might cram some food down my throat, but never having much of an appetite, I usually skipped breakfast. Then I headed to the hospital, where faith and doubt did battle. My midday break might be a trip to the coffee shop, or perhaps a jaunt downstairs to the cafeteria where I had a patty melt with the rye bread cooked in about a stick of butter. Though I could not really enjoy food at the time, the patty melt dripping in grease provided me some "comfort food therapy." From there, I looked forward to the evening, when I spent time with Grace, Isaiah, and Noah.

With the help of this technique, I did not break, but kept upright despite the terrible winds. This is not to say that I made it through every moment with the utmost grace and dignity. There is a fist-sized hole in my bedroom door that is a daily reminder to me of my occasional loss of control. But I did survive, and that was all I needed to do.

There were people who told me how amazed they were at my strength. Though these statements were flattering (especially to a former Marine who liked to envision himself as a sturdy, unyielding fortress), the fact of the matter was that personal strength had very little to do with me staying upright. I was not strong. I was blessed—unbelievably blessed.

Now, you have to understand that I don't use the word "blessing" lightly. In fact, it is incredibly ironic that I might be writing a book that would be talking about God at all. You see, as a young man, I was agnostic bordering on all-out atheist. I, to put it bluntly, believed that religion was a crutch that self-deluded people chose to believe as truth in order to help them make it through the giant risk that life is. I viewed the faithful as sheep, blindly following the flock, not because they knew any better but because it was what everybody else did.

How I came to believe in God is a very long story for another book. Suffice it to say that, when I did find my faith, my vision of God ended up being a very personal one. I still view him in monotheistic terms and use the masculine pronouns when talking about him. But that has more to do with the Judeo-Christian culture in which I was raised. I know that an omnipotent God can present himself in any way he sees fit. So I can imagine that he might want to present himself to Hindus as multiple gods, or to Christians as an incredibly ripped old guy with a white beard, or to wiccans as the spirits of the natural world. As for how he wants us to live our lives, there is only one rule I am certain of. Many call it the Golden Rule: Do unto others as you would have them do unto you.

Now, if you live by this rule, does it mean that you will live a life devoid of pain and grief and sometimes even despair? No, I'm afraid not. And I believe this is why: though I believe in an all-powerful God, I do not believe that God causes bad things to happen. He may have created the world where bad things *can* happen, but that is where his involvement in it ends. Bad things (earthquakes, tsunamis, car accidents, pulmonary embolisms) are a cost of living. They are a part of being in this world that God created and are as unavoidable as all the good things in life.

This is why I have always hated the saying, "God only gives you what you can handle." I hate the saying, 1) because it's one of those things people say without thinking, and 2) because life gives people more than they can handle all the time.

Life will back up a dump truck full of shit and bury you in it. It is when you are buried in that heap of shit, trying desperately to find the will and the energy to survive, that God comes into play. It is when you are eyeballs deep in it that you find out whether you are blessed or not. If you have been a good person, if you have lived a good life, if you have reached out to help others and done unto them as you would have them do unto you, then when that dump truck backs up, as it so often will, you will have family and friends there, willing to grab a shovel, roll up their sleeves, and get knee-deep in a pile of shit to dig you out.

On December 2, 2009, it was my and my family's, turn for life to back up the dump truck and bury us. And, once again, God did his work in our lives through his creations. It was as I walked through "the valley of the shadow of death" that every nice thing I had ever done in my life was repaid tenfold. As I walked through that darkness, his rod and his staff were the thousands of people that, on December 3 and in the days that followed, got to work to get me and my family out. When I tell you I was not strong, I was blessed—this is what I am talking about.

My first great blessing was, of course, our family. My parents, who were in town in anticipation of Anthony's arrival, were invaluable when it came to taking care of the kids while I was busy at the hospital. They also took care of the multitude of household tasks that come with a large family. Beyond that, they managed to still get new wood floors installed in our home.

We had already planned to get rid of all our carpet in anticipation of "lung issues" that preemies are prone to. After Brynn's embolism, we almost canceled the job entirely. My parents did not let that happen. Though it meant the kids and I would sleep together on a mattress in the living room, they forged ahead with the plans, making sure our home was ready for their newest grandchild.

My sister had just gone back to her home in Indianapolis after also coming out west to help us prepare for Anthony. She offered to get on a plane and come right back. Fortunately, we would not need her to do so. Alan, Holly, and Katie were all my teammates in hospital life. When I was not able to be there, either with Brynn or with Anthony, they were there, reading to Brynn, listening to doctors, holding the baby, while their own faith and doubts did battle. Beyond our immediate family there were uncles, aunts, cousins, lifelong friends, too numerous to list, who all came together to help us with whatever needed doing.

Another of my great blessings came the day after Brynn's embolism in the form of an email from the owner of Vironex. It was sent to my boss and then forwarded to me. It read as follows:

Todd [my boss],

Effective 12/1, Kelley will convert Kyle to salary...so he does not have to worry about hours and pay. Anything at all that we can do, please let me know right away. Thanks.

Alan (owner of company)

I don't think I have to explain how amazing this was. I thought I might actually have to leave my job to care for my family. Instead, my company was going to pay me to take care of my family.

Our financial situation was the third greatest worry on my mind, after Brynn and Anthony. That single email almost entirely eliminated that burden. It is an act for which I will be forever grateful. This was just the beginning. News about Brynn's condition spread at an unimaginable speed. First, there was Facebook. Posts on my Facebook page were posted, then reposted, and reposted again. Before the week was out, friends of friends of friends (people I had never met in my entire life) were reposting my status. From those posts, prayer circles from across the country were notified—then across the world.

Besides my own Facebook page, Brynn's dad, Alan, sent regular emails to a large number of friends regarding Brynn, keeping people up to date and requesting prayers. Then, our friend Dawn Dahlberg set up a blog that was essentially my Facebook postings reposted.

When all was said and done, prayers, good thoughts, and love were being sent toward our family from thousands of people from multiple faiths from all over the world. Christians of all denominations, Buddhists in China, priests in Africa, and friends and family from every faith under the sun sent their love our way.

I began to joke that my goal was to bug God with so many prayers from so many different people that out of sheer annoyance he would give back my wife to me. In reality, it was only a half joke. Having no idea how to get a miracle, I figured I'd try whatever I could, and thousands of prayers seemed like a good start.

Love and prayers, though they were the greatest blessings we received, were not the only blessings. The blog that Dawn created was set up to receive donations. Through that, we received many donations from friends, family, and total strangers. This further decreased my fears about our finances. This money was a cushion in the early months and was later used to cover many things that insurance did not.

Grace's elementary school also did a collection for our family from which we received gift cards for local restaurants, cash, and checks. Of all the gifts we received, my personal favorite came in this collection. It was a blue envelope—a bill-paying envelope for a dental office. The office address had been scratched out and in child's writing it said: **For Grace.** Under the scratched-out address with an arrow drawn up to her first name it read **Ervin $3.** Inside the envelope were two dollar bills folded together and four quarters.

Receiving charity from a child is a humbling and lovely experience. The memory of it still brings me great joy.

Another favorite: one night we heard a knock at our door. When my dad answered it, he saw somebody running down the street. Left on our porch was a simple Mason jar filled with coins. Inside, the note read: "Every year we collect our spare change in a jar, giving it to a family in need. This year we have chosen you. God Bless." I liked this idea so much that now I have a giving jar on our counter, collecting all of our spare change as well.

Then there was the food. Oh my God, was there food! It seems that the first thing that people want to do for you when tragedy strikes is to provide you with a home-cooked meal. It is evidence of how blessed we are that, at one point, I had so much food delivered to my house that I had both of my kitchen countertops, my entire fridge, my freezer in the garage, AND an ice chest filled with food. It was then that I realized that managing all of the goodwill coming our way was going to be a full-time job.

Luckily, I had two dear people who helped me greatly in this regard. First, Laura Macias, a fellow teacher of Brynn's at Sierra Vista, coordinated everything coming our way from the school, and also disseminated information to all of Brynn's coworkers who were worried about her. Then our dear friend Libby Vice (the wife of my old college roommate, Tommy) managed everything else. These two women, who had never known each other prior to this, worked together to organize work parties to come to our house, gathered donations, and hundreds of other tasks. They were amazing and, when I talk about blessings, they were two of my greatest. We received help from so many people in so many ways that saying thank you to all of them became impossible.

I have always believed, despite all the news we hear to the contrary, that there are more good people out there than there are bad ones. The deluge of help our family received, from all backgrounds, ages, and faiths during this most trying time, confirmed my belief. The vast majority of people are good, and good people are a blessing to us all. And for the blessings my family received, I am grateful beyond imagination. *Thy rod and thy staff, they comfort me.*

CHAPTER FIFTEEN
A Christmas Miracle?

1. Make the Sign of the Cross and say
    the Apostles Creed.
2. Say the Our Father.
3. Say three Hail Marys.
4. Say the Glory be to the Father.
5. Announce the first mystery; then say the Our Father.
6. Say ten Hail Marys while meditating on
    the mystery.
7. Say the Glory be to the Father.
8. Announce the second mystery; then say the Our
    Father. Repeat 6 and 7 and continue with third,
    fourth, and fifth mysteries in the same manner.

The above series is the order for how to pray the Catholic rosary. The whole process takes about twenty to thirty minutes or so, depending on how fast you can pray. In eight years of being married to a Catholic, I've learned that Catholics pray the rosary for any number of events.

For my wife, my in-laws, and many other Catholics, the rosary brings comfort and solace when times are difficult. For me, the poster child for attention deficit disorder, the rosary is a special kind of torture—twenty to thirty minutes of repetitive droning that, as soon as it begins, I begin to sigh heavily and wonder when it will be over.

On the night of December 9, when I walked into my wife's room, I was in for quite a treat. Unbeknownst to me, one of Brynn's friends had asked a member of her church to come and pray the rosary over Brynn. This lady who came to pray apparently had some track record with healing. I just happened to show up in time for the prayer circle.

Along with me in the room were Phaidra's mom (Jeri, who had made a habit of coming to Brynn's room almost every night), Brynn's sister Katie, and Brynn's mom and dad (who had come to meet the lady who was leading the prayer).

Have you ever been stuck on a plane, and all you want to do is close your eyes and take a nap, but you happen to be sitting next to the guy who can't stop talking? This is pretty much how I felt when this lady I had never met before asked me if I would join in the prayer. I wanted to say, "That's okay, you can leave me out." But that would have been way too rude.

I looked over at Jeri, who is also not Catholic and who, consequently, also had the *That's okay, you can leave me out* look on her face. We smiled at each other, knowing we were stuck, and held hands in a circle as the woman began the rosary.

I held Jeri's hand with my left hand and put my right on Brynn. The lady began to pray and, almost instantly, I began to sigh deeply and wonder when it would be over. Then, out of nowhere, interjected in between the normal prayers, she began to utter a series of sibilant noises, sounding something like a snake hissing.

I was taken aback at first. I looked over at her, confused for a moment, until it hit me—*She's speaking in tongues! Are you kidding me? She speaking in freaking tongues!*

Every cynical bone in my body urged me to stop the

farce immediately by saying exactly what I was think-ing. Then another thought ran through my mind, *Kyle, quit thinking that you know it all. You don't. You don't know how God works. So far, you have been open to every prayer, every good thought, and every ounce of positive energy that thousands of people from every faith imaginable have sent your way. Maybe this lady IS speaking in tongues. Maybe she's a nutcase. The fact is, she's here to help your wife either way. Take it. For whatever it's worth, take it.*

I did take it. And in that instant, when I had chucked away my cynicism if only for a moment, I figured I would have a few words with God myself. My right hand still rested on my wife's forehead. In my mind I reached out to that greatness, that positive energy, that hugeness that I call God; I opened myself up completely. *If there is any way, any way at all that you can use me to heal her, please, do it. I am open to it. If only for this mo-ment I will believe in the ridiculous, I will believe in the impossible.*

And for a moment, I *believed* that his energy was passing through me, into her brain, and fixing what was damaged. Call it chi, or life force, or the Holy Spirit; call it whatever you like. I know I didn't care about theologi-cal semantics at the time. All I knew is that I was willing to try anything to save my wife, and if that meant that I had to believe in miracles, then I would.

I would love to be able to say that the next day I came into the hospital to find my wife awake, talking—the exact person I had lost, back as quickly, as instantly as I had lost her. The truth, however, is that the journey through the valley of the shadow of death was a long, slow, incremental, and emotionally jarring process.

I had wonderful moments, like the one not long after I told Brynn to not be afraid to do something amazing without me. I walked into her room and there she was, looking at her mother—really looking at her! Her eyes were dazed, but she was definitely looking at her.

Elated, exultant, jubilant, ecstatic, euphoric, there are multiple words meant to describe how I felt, seeing my wife, with her eyes open, looking at her mother. None of those words come close to what I felt. As a writer, it shames me to say that I cannot describe it. It was simply the best feeling ever. Then, Fear crept in, using doubt as his tool. My good mood was replaced by the inevitable questions—*Is this it? Is this the dreaded "plateau"? Is this as far as she will go?*

There was no way of knowing. In fact, the professionals told me that my feelings of elation were unfounded. They told me that she was in a coma with her eyes open.

The "plateau" was the single most terrifying thought in the entire ordeal. The plateau was a place somewhere between healing and death in which Brynn might not only require constant care, but she might never recognize me or her children. The woman I love not recognizing me, and therefore not loving me, scared the crap out of me. *Either take her or heal her, but none of this middle-of-the-road bullshit.*

There is a term that is often used to describe this type of emotional up and down. People call it an emotional roller coaster. For me, it was more like an emotional Richter scale and my life was a 9.0.

I was caught in a tug-of-war between hope and despair, and due to the up-and-down nature of my emotional state, it is very hard to pinpoint a time that I can definitively say that hope began to win. If I had to, at gunpoint, I would say it was a day or so after I saw her looking at her mom. It was a little over a week after her incident, still very early on. At this point, the doctors were still very negative. I came into her room and, sure enough, she had her eyes open. She was still staring off rather blankly into space, but I could see a remnant of the spark that is my Brynn somewhere behind those pupils. I decided to ask her a question. First I had to explain the rule. It was the rule I had seen in a hundred movies about coma patients: a blink meant yes.

I explained the rule and then asked the question, "Would you like to listen to some music?"

She, ever so slowly, as though she were putting every ounce of her mental energy into it, closed her eyes.

I about jumped out of the room. I was so excited, I decided to run with it and I asked her a second question. "How about some Black Eyed Peas?" Brynn loves the Black Eyed Peas.

Again, she strained to give me the world's slowest blink. That was all—a couple of blinks. But what those blinks meant was that she was still in there, fighting to make her way out. My Brynn wanted to listen to music. My Brynn wanted some Black Eyed Peas.

I walked over to the little speaker we had for her iPod, found the Black Eyed Peas *Hey Mama* and turned it up nice and loud.

The lyrics echoed throughout the CVU as I celebrated the world's slowest eye blink, sharing the news with anyone who poked a head in the door to see what the racket was about.

From that point on, I viewed Brynn's recovery as though her brain was a computer that was simply rebooting. With every day that passed, new systems came online. As they did, I needed to be prepared and ensure that she had all the advantages modern medicine could provide her. I didn't exactly ignore what the doctors were telling me, but I did not let their opinions sway my mood so drastically. Two eye blinks were enough for me to believe she could find her way out of it. Two eye blinks showed purpose, and Brynn with a purpose is something to behold.

I began to scour the Internet and the bookstore, trying to find any and all information I could about recovering from brain damage. I learned that one of the biggest problems for patients recovering from an extensive coma was that their joints literally froze up and were never again functional. I requested a physical therapist to come to the room and show us how to keep Brynn's joints flexible.

One of Brynn's incredible nurses, Anne Morkaut, sat through the lesson with us, learning the exercises and then working Brynn's joints when we were not able to. This was not part of her job. This was just something she did because she was a great nurse. *Your rod and your staff, they comfort me.*

On the Internet, I learned that because Brynn was so young, and because she was such a smart and determined person prior to her event, she had the absolute best chance possible of recovery. I also learned that "recovery" had a very broad definition. After what Brynn had gone through, she would be exceedingly lucky to be able to dress herself again.

A few days after Brynn blinked to listen to the Black Eyed Peas, on December 16, I was in the NICU holding my son, trying desperately to get his bottle in him before the twenty-minute time limit. Brynn's mom came into the NICU very excited. She had just run up from the CVU. "She smiled!" She started the story with the end. "Can you believe it? She smiled!" We hugged in celebration of the news and she went on to explain, "Shari and Dr. Wu and some others were there, and you know Shari…"

Shari, it needs to be said here, was one of Brynn's nurses from Labor and Delivery. She, like Brynn, is a very loquacious person and the two of them had hit it off, spending many hours chatting and becoming friends in the two weeks that Brynn was on bedrest. When Brynn suffered her embolism, Shari was one of the faces in scrubs at her room. I remember how distraught she was, and I remember her distress being one of my major clues that *Yes, this was happening to me.*

"You know, Shari...," Brynn's mom went on, "She came in and was just chatting with Brynn, telling her how they were referring to Anthony as Benjamin Button because he looked like a little old man, and Brynn smiled! And then, she told her how you said that was fine as long as he ended up looking like Brad Pitt, and she smiled even bigger!"

I blinked away the tears of joy that wetted my eyes. This was the best news I had heard yet. Neurologically speaking, an appropriate response to humor was a great indicator that she might pull through. More importantly for me, though, was the knowledge that my girl's sense of humor was intact.

I wholeheartedly believe that the biggest reason Brynn fell in love with me is because I could make her smile. *If she can smile, she can still love me, even if she needs to learn to love me all over again. If I can make her smile, I've got a chance.*

And yet, I could not help but feel a little disappointed because I had not been there to see it. Then my own words came back to me—*Don't be afraid to do something amazing without me.*

The news of her smile spread throughout the hospital quickly. As I walked the halls that day, I was stopped by familiar faces in scrubs and they asked me, "Did you hear? She smiled!"

To this day, I am a little surprised they didn't announce it over the hospital PA system. "Attention all hospital personnel, Brynn Ervin smiled at a joke today—Just thought you'd like to know." It was a momentous step in her recovery and a tremendous bright spot for all of those who were cheering her on.

Two days after her first smile, on December 18, I came into the hospital to find that she had finally had a tracheostomy done. This is a procedure in which they cut a hole into the trachea so that they can insert the ventilator tube straight into the trachea as opposed to going through the mouth. We had been looking forward to the tracheostomy for days. The tube sticking out of her throat was somewhat grotesque, but we considered it a much better and more comfortable situation for Brynn than having the tubes in her mouth.

The "trach" came with the added benefit that I could then kiss my wife on her lips for the very first time since her event. When I did, she, very clumsily, like a movie zombie, put her arms straight up into the air.

"Hey!" I said, very excited. And though it was impossible to decipher exactly what she wanted based on her rudimentary motions, as her husband, I took it upon myself to make some assumptions. "I'm going to take that to mean that you need a hug."

Being very careful not to mess with all of her tubes, I put her arms around my back and hugged her. I held her in my arms, squeezing her ever so gently and again breathed in her scent.

It's strange, but before her embolism, I did not even know that I knew what she smelled like. After her embolism, breathing in her scent was like breathing in mild barbiturates, instantly lowering my heart rate and blood pressure, reassuring me on a primal level that my wife was still alive. It was incredibly intoxicating.

After a kiss and a hug, she gave me a real treat. I said something stupid, trying to be funny, and my wife smiled at me. It was not quite that "Brynn" smile that reaches her eyes, but that simple expression of pleasure on my wife's face was quite possibly the most remarkable thing I have ever seen in my life. *If she smiles at me, I've got a chance.*

Soon thereafter, Brynn was moved from the CVU to the ICU. The nurses who had given her the nickname Sleeping Beauty fought to keep this patient that they had become so close to. But the CVU was filling up. Brynn was now much more stable and was no longer, technically speaking, a cardio patient. In my mind, what this move meant was that the risk of her death was now minimal. From this point on, things were going to be measured in terms of her recovery.

It's very difficult for me to explain my emotional state during this time. Though she was smiling at me, and responding to humor, she was still in a precarious position. She could not speak; she was still dependant on the ventilator to help her breathe; she could not scratch her nose if she had an itch. Yet I was happy. A smile was so much more than I ever expected. Everything else was butter.

This is not to say that there weren't difficult times. Only the very next day, I spent two hours holding Brynn's right arm down because she kept raising it up to her head in an apparent attempt to dislodge her respirator tubes.

"Baby, you gotta keep your arm down. Come on. Keep it down here. You're going to rip out your tubes." At this point I'd like you to recall Brynn's pathological stubbornness that I've mentioned before. She just kept raising her arm, tangling it in the tubes, and pulling her blood oxygen sensor off of her finger, causing the alarm to go off.

This was one of the very few occasions that I was not entirely happy with her care. I had asked for them to sedate her so that she could get some rest, but they were unwilling to. Sedatives would mask any neurological improvements. But I had learned that rest was the most important factor in recovering from a brain injury, and this was not at all restful.

Furthermore, I could not sit by her bed all day, trying

to keep her from tearing her tubes out. Finally, after several hours of this, I gave up trying and just sat down by her bed.

Sure enough, not five minutes later, Brynn, stubborn as ever, succeeded in pulling the respirator tube off of the plastic fitting that was stitched to the hole in her neck. The respirator alarm went off and her nurse rushed in.

Her nurse was not overly pleased with this development, but I just shrugged. *You try and stop her,* I thought to myself, *brain damage or not, she's one stubborn broad.*

It wasn't all struggle though, either. There were even moments of "fun." Yes—it is possible to have fun in an intensive care unit. It may not be likely, but it is possible.

One such moment was the day Brynn's bed malfunctioned. Her bed was a very complex piece of equipment with a mattress that was essentially a big air cushion. It was designed this way to prevent bedsores. One of the features of this mattress was that it could rapidly deflate, lowering the patient to the stiff surface beneath should CPR ever be required.

One afternoon, I was standing next to her bed, talking to her when the mattress suddenly began to deflate. Both Brynn and I were startled as the air whooshed out of the release valve sounding like a giant balloon letting go of its air. Her eyes got wide as she sank into the collapsing mattress like a hot dog in a bun.

Soon, all the air was out of the mattress and Brynn was lying on the bed's hard under-surface. She could not speak with her mouth, but her wide eyes and her raised eyebrows were saying, *Oh shit, I just broke my bed!*

I looked at her, smiled and said, "Weeeeeeeeee!" as though she had just been on an amusement park ride. She smiled back and the nurse came in to fix her bed.

By December 21, Brynn's respiratory situation had

improved enough that the doctors wanted to try to take her off the ventilator. If she could maintain her blood oxygen levels on her own, she would stay off the ventilator and be one step closer to an existence outside of hospital care.

This was a great step, but it came with problems of its own. Instead of the ventilator helping her to breathe, she now had an oxygen mask sitting over the hole in her trachea. The oxygen was much dryer than the air from the ventilator had been. This caused the mucus in her throat to harden and then plug her airway, causing horrible coughing fits.

When she started coughing, I cringed in terror. I knew it meant she would need to be suctioned soon. I sat there and prayed that she would be able to cough up whatever was down there on her own. When she could not, I had to go get the nurse to call the respiratory tech.

As Brynn's cognition improved, her response to suctioning worsened. When the tech advanced the tube, she started coughing spastically and her face became bright red. Even after they retracted the tube, she coughed for minutes on end.

Beyond the choking sensation, there was also the fact that her sternum had been sawed open for her heart surgery, and she probably had several cracked ribs from ninety-five minutes of CPR, so every cough was excruciating. It was probably the most painful thing Brynn had to endure, and standing there watching her endure it was the hardest thing I had to do during her entire hospital stay. With the oxygen now drying out the mucus in her throat, she needed to be suctioned many more times every day.

The day after Brynn was removed from the ventilator, just three days before Christmas, I was certain I was going to hear from some news reporter or another asking to interview the husband of the "Christmas Miracle" at Anaheim Regional Medical Center. The reason I was so sure of this was because, on December 22, one of the hospital's physical therapists came in and got Brynn sitting up—on her own!

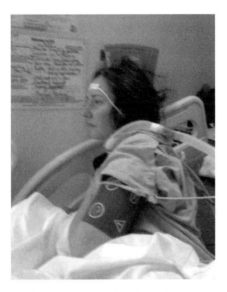

Brynn Sitting Up for the First Time

She was able to stay upright for fifteen minutes. I was sure that the news media was going to get a hold of this story and run it on Christmas Day. I never was contacted by the news media (well, at least not for a Christmas story), but after Brynn sat up, I heard "our Christmas miracle" being bandied about all over the hospital.

Because Christmas was fast approaching, some members of the hospital staff pulled some strings and gave me the opportunity to bring the kids in to see Brynn. Deciding whether or not to take them up on this offer was one of the more difficult decisions I had to make. Brynn was still in very bad shape. She could not speak.

She had almost no motor control. She was in and out of consciousness, and when she was awake, she was usually either dazed or crying with discomfort. I questioned whether bringing the kids to see their mother this way was wise.

In the end I decided to bring them to see her. Though she was much more stable than she had been, she still had a persistent fever, and death from infection was a very real risk. If she were to die, I wanted the kids to have had the opportunity to see their mom one last time. Beyond that, I wanted to see if the sight of her children might spur some further cognitive recovery. So, on December 23, I brought Grace, Isaiah, and Noah to the hospital. We walked into the waiting room and then to the guard desk.

I bent down to speak to my kids, making eye contact with each of them so that they would know that Dad was serious. "Okay. We're going to go see Momma right now. She's still very sick and will probably be asleep. I need for you to be very quiet—whispers only." I accentuated the last words. "So what's the rule?"

All three of them answered in unison, "Whispers only."

"Great. All right, keep your hands in your pockets until we get to Mom's room. When we get there we will wash our hands really, really good with hand sanitizer. What's the rule?"

"Hands in our pockets," they all answered.

"After we wash our hands, then we can hug and kiss Mommy. Okay?"

"Okay."

Brynn wasn't sleeping when we got there. Knowing we were coming with the kids, the physical therapist that helped her sit up before got her up in a chair next to her bed.

It had been a month since the children had seen their mother, and it was not the reunion I hoped for. Yes,

Brynn was sitting there and her eyes were open, but she was not in the room. She stared off blankly into nowhere. I don't think she even realized we were there.

Grace, probably recognizing her mother's spaced-out expression, as well as exhibiting the same fear of all the machinery that I did when I first saw Brynn, was reluctant to get close. She went and stood by Brynn's legs, but she did not want to get up in her lap or on the bed next to her.

I'm not sure Noah even really recognized who she was. This woman with the blank stare was not the mother he knew—the mother who could convey whole paragraphs of meaning with a single facial expression. We tried to put him on her lap, but he hesitated.

Isaiah, though, my deep river, climbed up onto the bed and gave his mom a kiss and a hug. He, ever so gently, touched her face and kissed her again. It was all at once, wonderful, heartwarming, and intensely sad. It was going to be a very difficult Christmas.

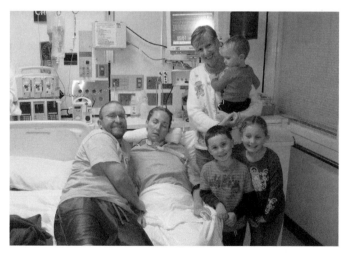

The Ervin Kids Visiting Their Mom for the First Time

The next day was Christmas Eve and, like every other day of that time period, it was filled with wonderful moments and very difficult moments. On the wonderful side, knowing that I was unable to get Christmas shopping done, the nurses from Labor and Delivery, Postpartum, the ICU, NICU, and CVU all adopted an Ervin family member to get Christmas presents for. Those gifts were delivered on Christmas Eve and, MY GOD, did they spoil us. It was a stunning and beautiful display of generosity.

On the difficult side, I had to spend more and more time at Brynn's bedside, managing her care. Her incident with pulling out the ventilator tube had just been the beginning of a very tough period of her recovery. As her cognition improved, yes, we were treated to more smiles and it became apparent that she realized we were there, but it also brought new problems. These problems stemmed from the fact that she was now becoming aware of her situation and, unfortunately, her discomfort.

Two days prior to Christmas Eve, Brynn picked up the rather strange habit of kicking her leg into the air over and over again. She did this continually for hours on end. The kicking was so incessant that one of the nurses dubbed her a Rockette. She simply did not stop kicking, not even to sleep. She stayed awake, all night long, kicking her legs.

By Christmas Eve, Brynn had not really slept at all for several days. This troubled me greatly. Again, I wanted for the doctors to prescribe something to get her to sleep, but again they were reluctant. This was incredibly frustrating for both her family and the nursing staff, because it was not just that she was kicking. She also kept getting her leg stuck between the bed rails. Time and again, we fixed it, putting it back on the bed, only to have her get it stuck again minutes later.

The kicking was so repetitive that I felt like she was trying to talk to us, but we could not understand the language. I was certain she was upset by something, but I did not know what it was. It was like trying to communicate with a very bad mime.

I wanted to fix the thing bothering her. I could not. I wanted to break things in frustration until I finally figured it out.

After she had gotten her leg stuck for the umpteenth time that day, one of her socks came off her foot. I started to put it back on when I realized that the skin on her foot was incredibly calloused and dry and cracking, a result of the extensive swelling and then shrinking that her body had gone through. I imagined the cracking skin must be uncomfortable, and I asked the nurse if there was some lotion I could use. When she brought me some, I began to rub it into Brynn's feet. Within two minutes, she was sleeping. Finally, after two days of what must have been maddening itchiness, she finally had some relief—so did I.

With the utmost pleasure, I rubbed lotion into my wife's feet, because now I could *finally* do something to make her feel better. After getting her to sleep, I went upstairs to visit Anthony for a while, but then made the mistake of trying to say good night to Brynn on my way out of the hospital. When I got to her room, she was no longer sleeping. Again, she was very obviously uncomfortable. I tried massaging some lotion into her feet, but that did not work as well as before. She did seem more comfortable, but she did not fall back to sleep. It was already very late, and I was exhausted.

"Baby, I'm going to go home to the kids now. Can you try and go to sleep? Close your eyes and try to rest."

She looked me in the eyes, a look of abject terror on

her face, and began to cry.

"Oh, no—don't cry," I pleaded with her, "Don't cry. I'll stay, okay. I'll stay until you fall asleep."

Fortunately, that got her to stop crying. Unfortunately, I was there at her bedside until 2:00 a.m. when she finally dozed off.

After going home for a short and fitful sleep, I awoke to excited children crawling all over our makeshift bed on the living room floor.

Trying to maintain some semblance of normalcy, my mom had purchased a Christmas tree that now stood only four feet from where we slept. Piled under it, about two-feet deep, were all of the gifts from the hospital staff.

I sent the kids out to my parents' trailer to wake them up and then crawled out from under the covers. I got myself a cup of coffee and looked forward to watching the kids open their plethora of gifts.

Not too long after I awoke, Brynn's mom called to tell me that she and Brynn's sister were sick and didn't want to risk spreading infection at the hospital. They would not be able to go to her that day. It was all up to me.

After that call, I tried to enjoy Christmas morning around the tree with my children, but it was impossible. All I could think of was how uncomfortable Brynn must be and that if she was awake, she must feel incredibly alone. I imagined having an itch I could not scratch. I imagined how I might feel if my wife did not come to me and scratch it. The thought made my chest tighten with anxiety, and my breathing became shallow.

As my children opened gifts, I buried my head in a blanket and tried to fight off the anxiety. I tried to enjoy the morning, but the anxiety would not go away. After the night I had just had with Brynn, there was no way I could leave her without someone at her bedside, especially on Christmas Day. Unable to tolerate the anxiety any further, I came out from underneath the blankets and said in a single breath, "I've got to go to the hospital. I have to go be with Brynn."

My parents didn't question me at all. They didn't ask me why I had buried myself in the covers. They didn't ask if I didn't want to stay and watch the kids unwrap their gifts.

"We've got the kids," they said. "You go ahead."

I left my kids with my parents and took off to the hospital.

There is a part of me that would love to tell this story as a Christmas miracle. But from my point of view, I just can't. Though the timing is close, the fact of the matter is that December 25, 2009, was the single worst Christmas of my entire life.

I don't remember much about it. All I remember is that it was a horrible, frustrating, anxiety-filled day in which I was stuck at my wife's bedside yet unable to help her feel even remotely more comfortable. Yes, things were better than they had been, but it would be several more days before I felt that we were truly on the other side of the Valley.

Three days after Christmas, I was sitting at Brynn's bedside trying to get her to smile. I wanted to take a picture of her smiling to put it on Facebook. She wouldn't smile.

I looked her in the eyes. "Come on, smile for me."

She looked back at me. Her mouth moved in what looked like an attempt to say something.

I was stunned. "Are you trying to say something?"

She looked at me, confused. And her mouth did the same thing. But again a look of confusion and frustration came to her face. It seemed to say, *I know how to do this. Why can't I do this?*

I was certain that she was trying to say something. I thought she might be saying "cold," but the tracheostomy prevented her from being able to vocalize, and because I can't read lips, I couldn't be sure. I tried to think of a word that she might say that would be easy for me to lip read, so that I could know for certain that she was trying to talk. "Say 'mom,'" I told her.

Her lips came together ever so slowly, then apart for the "O" and then back together again for the final "M."

"Oh, baby, that's huge! That is so huge! Are you cold? Is that what you were saying before?"

She nodded.

"Nurse!" I shouted across the ICU. "She's cold! She just *told* me she's cold. Can we get a warm blanket?"

"Yes, of course." Her nurse was almost as pleased as I was. "I'll get one right away."

"Baby, you can't talk. You have a tube in your throat."

She reached up probably meaning to touch her throat, but she had absolutely no fine motor control, so her arm flailed over her head.

"Don't worry about that, sweetness. We've got a long road ahead before we get that out. But I'm here with you! Okay, I'm here with you."

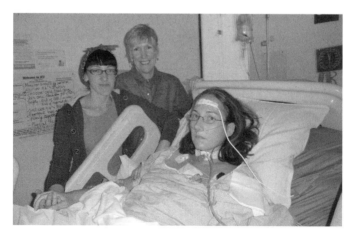

Katie Sanchez, Holly Holderness, and Brynn

After that, Brynn's recovery really began to pick up steam. The very next day, only four days after that horrible Christmas, I was on my way to the hospital when I received a call on my cell phone. My caller ID showed that it was Phaidra. She was calling from the hospital.

"Hey, Phaidra."

"Where are you?" she asked excitedly

"On my way. Why?"

"Hurry up and get over here. She wants to see him!" I instantly knew what she meant. Brynn wanted to see Anthony.

"I just parked. I'm on my way in!" I hung up the phone, excited by the news. Then it hit me. Phaidra had said, "She wants to see him." *But how…*

I called Phaidra back. "What did you mean she wants to see him?"

"She told me! She said, 'I want to see him.'!"

I don't remember what I said after that. I just remember feeling the most intense sense of relief.

That very same day, two of the hospital's physical therapists came to her room, got her out of the bed, stood her up, and, with the help of the rolling bed table, raised as high as it would go so that she could lean on it, got her walking.

I was now, finally, on the other side of "the valley of the shadow of death" and feeling the light on my skin felt good, oh so good.

CHAPTER SIXTEEN
Happily Ever After

Due to fear of infection, Brynn did not get to see Anthony on the day she asked to see him. But the next day, Wednesday, December 30, things changed.

Having stood up on her own and talked, Brynn reached the point that she was now going to be transferred to a rehabilitation hospital. Furthermore, Anthony was going to be discharged the very same day.

The staff of the CVU, the NICU, and the ICU were not going to let these two patients leave that hospital until Brynn had seen little baby Anthony. The NICU nurses wheeled Anthony downstairs in a portable incubator, keeping him protected as they brought him into the ICU.

Word had spread throughout the hospital and, despite the strict ICU rules, when the nurses arrived with the baby, there were some ten or more hospital staff gathered around Brynn's bed, waiting.

One of the nurses opened the incubator, picked up his tiny swaddled body, and placed him right next to Brynn. He rested there in the crook of her arm, and snuggled up to her face.

Brynn's cognitive abilities were still far from great. She still had something of a blank stare in her eyes. But as her son nuzzled up against her, she smiled.

Mother and Son Finally Together

Sniffles filled the room as doctors, nurses, techs, and family all fought back the gathering tears.

The pulmonologist who had overseen Brynn's care from pretty much the moment the clot struck was there. He came into the room with a great smile on his face, and walked up to the side of Brynn's bed where I was standing. "Hello, Brynn," he said, the smile never leaving his face. "How are you?"

Brynn did not respond other than to look at him.

He persisted, "Do you know who this is?" he said, referring to me. "Can you tell me who this guy is standing next to you?"

She was very slow to answer. A look of puzzlement came over her face. She struggled but could not come up with the words "husband" or "Kyle." She said what fit best from the words that she could find in her damaged mind, "My best friend."

***

Sometime shortly after Brynn's transfer to the rehab hospital, Katie and her husband, Andy, in an incredibly courageous act of familial love, moved in to help with the baby. They squeezed themselves into Grace's bedroom, while Grace moved in with her brothers, and have lived in our home for over a year, helping to get the kids to school, the laundry done, the family fed, and any number of other tasks that we could not have accomplished without them. They have essentially sacrificed a year of their lives for the betterment of my family—a debt I doubt I will ever be able to repay.

Andrew Sanchez, Katie Sanchez and the Ervin Family at the Completion of Anthony's Baptismal Rite

***

Vironex, the company I work for, continues to be incredibly flexible with me and my schedule. I am back at work, but I am still operating at a fraction of the capacity I once did.

Yes, every single day presents us with extraordinary challenges. Though Brynn has made stunning progress, she is still very limited in what she can do. Simply doing the laundry is impossible for her because she cannot carry the clothes out to the garage.

Anthony has battled numerous infections (far more than any of his brothers or sister) and made his way through the gambit of antibiotics. But when I look at my life, even with all its new challenges, I cannot help but feel insanely blessed.

Brynn, after months of hard work and therapy, cannot only dress herself and tie her own shoes—she can now drive a car, walk with a walker, and do any number of other things that were at one time considered absolutely impossible. Many people would be hard-pressed to tell that she has any brain injury at all.

Anthony has grown from a tiny doll-like child into a vigorous toddler who loves to wrestle on the living room floor with his two older brothers.

I cannot explain what it feels like to be granted not just one, but two incredible miracles. Out of the more than seven billion people on the planet, I am one—just one (well, the only one I know of) who has had the indescribable good fortune to watch his child that was supposed to die, not only live but come to thrive, *and* watch his wife go through ninety-five minutes of sustained cardiac arrest and, somehow, come out on the other side.

I have no idea why I got these miracles. I wish this could be a "How To" book—How To Get Your Miracle. Unfortunately, I have no idea why God chose us—none whatsoever.

We love God in our family but no more so than many families. He plays a central role in our lives, but is often relegated to the sidelines as we busy ourselves with making ends meet and taking care of the needs of a family. We sometimes forget to look to him. We sometimes find ourselves angry with him and our situation. We oftentimes don't understand why certain things happen in our lives. We don't go to church every Sunday. I wouldn't go at all, if it were up to me.

Brynn's parents are incredibly religious people. So maybe these are entirely their miracles, and I am just a lucky beneficiary. Maybe it is the simple fact that thousands and thousands of people were praying for us. Maybe it was the lady speaking in tongues. Maybe it was me placing my hand on her forehead and asking God to heal her through me, or maybe it was Anthony saying prayers in a language only babies know.

Here is the simple fact of the matter—I don't care. I don't care who gets the credit for the "why." I only care that God gets the credit for the "how."

There is no doubt that medical science had its fair place in all of this. I am so very thankful that a machine like the Arctic Sun exists, because I know that without it, my wife would be brain dead. But without divine intervention—without the exact right people in the exact right place, at the exact right time—medical science would not have had its chance. God gets the credit for that, God and God alone. Thank you, God. Thank you so very much.

BRYNN'S POINT OF VIEW

I don't remember any of it. From a couple of days before my embolism to sometime in late December, I have absolutely no memory. There was no white light, no tunnel, no heavenly voices calling to me. There is nothing—a complete blank.

When my memory did come back, it was spotty at best. It was like my "record" button was on only some of the time. So my memories jump all over the place.

My first memory was turning my face to the left to look at Jim and Carol Moak, friends of my parents from St. Louise De Marillac Church. I was wondering why my parents' friends were there. I was confused. Where was I, and why were they, of all people, at the edge of my bed?

"Hi, hon, you're awake," Carol said to me.

I was thinking to myself, *Of course I'm awake, why wouldn't I be?* I couldn't talk to them, but that didn't seem to concern me. Having been a teacher for ten years, talking constantly, you would think that not being able to talk would have been terrifying. You might think that would have sent up a big warning flag, but it didn't. I didn't even question it.

The very next thing I remembered (and this is where things get a little strange) was having this girl standing next to me. She had a deformity on her face. She was wearing a flowered T-shirt and jeans. She had jet-black hair and dark features. She reminded me of my students. I felt like she was ten years old. She was a part of a whole gang of kids that were all deformed in some way or another, and they were running around chasing each other, playing and having races on the rolling doctor's chairs. They were competing against each other. They raced up and down the hall and stopped to get water. Then they would drink it right in front of me, laughing. This girl in the flowered T-shirt taunted me with her water as a child might. All I wanted was some water, I put my hand out to grab the water, but she kept shaking her head no at me.

This memory, these deformed children that raced around my bed, taunting me, and who were invisible to everyone but me, were just as real to me as the memory of seeing Jim and Carol. In my mind they are the same and, if there are angels in my story, I believe these children were them. I believe this because these taunting children, strangely, brought me a solace that no person could. I wasn't worried because there were children there—children whose deformities made my own problems seem to pale in comparison. I thought to myself, it couldn't be that bad or they wouldn't be there. They understood me, though I could not talk, they told the nursing staff when I needed attention and stayed with me while the nurse took care of me. Their presence calmed me. Any cynic who reads this could easily put this memory on the multitude of drugs I was on or the damage my brain suffered, but I'm going with angels. Those kids stuck by my side until I left Anaheim Regional.

From Anaheim Regional, I was taken to a rehabilitation hospital. I remember odd things about the journey, but not the entire trip. I remember being rolled out the door, strapped down to a gurney. Someone placed a black sweater on me. A strange man told me that we were going for a little ride. And I didn't even question it. I trusted him. I knew he was going to take care of me. I didn't even question where my family was. I guess Kyle was in the front seat of the ambulance, but I didn't know that. If I couldn't see him, he wasn't there. I remember that the windshield wipers were on. I couldn't see them, but I must have heard them.

The next memory I had was the ambulance driver saying, "Oops, we ran a red light." I didn't even flinch. All my upbringing as a good driver, don't turn on a red light when the sign says "no turn on red," going the speed limit in school zones, etc., and I didn't even react that we broke the law.

After that I was in a strange room with miniblinds on the window. I glanced around the room to try and figure out where I was. There was no color anywhere. I glanced to my right and looked out the window, and instantly knew that it was New Year's Eve. I couldn't see a calendar, but could tell by the atmosphere. There was a party going on across the way. It was just like the movies. There were lights decorating the windows, party hats on people, champagne bursting open. I swear I could hear the bubbles fizzing. I heard the music drifting over the patio, and laughter. They appeared to be having a fabulous time. I thought to myself, *Someday I will go to a party like that*. Again, I didn't even question where my family was, I honestly can say I didn't know any better. I was all alone, and it didn't scare me.

Next, my mom and dad were with me, and I told them that I had to go potty. A nurse brought in a bedpan and everybody left the room. It was so uncomfortable, and the bowl was cutting into me, but no one could hear me when I called out that I was done. I didn't know about the call button. My mom came in and was so happy because "things were beginning to work." Only a mother could get so excited about pee and a moving bowel. I thought to myself, *She's crazy*.

My mom then showed me where the call button was

and how to use it. The only problem was that it was on my right side. For some reason, my right side was more affected by my embolism, and I couldn't use my right hand at all. I didn't have the strength to hold the button down. They tried moving the button to my left side, but then I could never find it, because it was out of my view and, again, if I couldn't see it, it wasn't there.

There was a steady stream of visitors. My sister's godparents (Kyle's old roommate Joshua Dowell's parents) came, all the way from Georgetown, California. I didn't even question why they came. Aunt Patty brought me Anthony's quilt. It was Paddington Bear. She showed me where his name was, but it just looked like squiggles to me. I instantly remembered the quilts that she had made for the other kids. I could picture Gracie's multi-colored quilt, Isaiah's alphabet quilt, and Noah's Noah's Ark quilt.

My uncle Bob came to see me. I asked him how marriage was. He had been remarried in the fall, and my family was ecstatic. I didn't go to the wedding, but I remembered. Remembering seemed to be very important to everybody, but I didn't understand why.

I didn't realize why I was there, what happened, or why people were crying all the time. They were tears of joy, but it confused me. It was when I saw my best friend, Phaidra, crying that I knew something really bad must have happened. In the thirty-something years I've known her, I've never seen her cry. She told me, "Don't you ever do that to me again. I almost lost you."

My first instinct was to comfort her. I reached for her and took her hand. It was the first time I thought about someone else beside myself.

When someone came into the room, I could only focus on that person. Everybody else would sort of disappear. So when another dear friend of mine came into the room, and I noticed who it was, despite the fact that

I was in a room full of people, I blurted out the first thing that came into my head. "Did you kick your husband to the curb yet?"

I didn't realize that she had poured her heart out to me about her rocky marriage when I was in a coma. I didn't even realize that I said it in front of everyone until Kyle chimed in. I was worried about my friend and only focused on her. Luckily, being the lady that she is, she brushed it off and said, "I thought you couldn't hear me."

The next moment, I reached for her pink phone. We had matching ones while we were teaching at the same school. I thought it was mine. Kyle said, "It's a good thing I didn't cancel your phone." *Why would he do that?* I asked him why and he told me that I couldn't press the buttons, so it was useless. I remember getting mad at him and telling him, "Hell, no!"

This is when he promised me my Coach purse. My friend encouraged this, she has a plethora of Coach bags. She was my witness and said, "I'll take you to get your purse."

All times of day, friends and family kept coming. I was excited to see everyone. If anybody I recognized walked into the room, I acted as if I hadn't seen the person in years, but in reality it was probably days, if not hours.

I remember Kyle finally got permission for me to sit outside on the patio. We spent hours there. I usually had a blanket on me. And I was always in yoga pants and a T-shirt. I refused to wear a bra. My aunt came and was looking all over for us and finally found us on the patio. The staff realized how much time we were spending out there and began to direct the visitors there. My cousin Karin came. She flew into San Diego, and she and her brother Jason came to see me. I wanted her cute boots and her jacket. Kyle said, "Well, she's back.

She wants boots."

I finally asked Kyle what happened, and that's when Kyle read me the Christmas letter. As I lay in my hospital bed with my husband lying next to me, I cried. It didn't happen. He was making it up. He wasn't telling the truth. I didn't believe him. He very sweetly told me that I had brain damage. I knew he was wrong. I didn't feel any different. I thought I would feel different, that I would know myself. But then he told me to move my right hand, and I didn't know which hand he meant. But I felt like me; I didn't feel like I had brain damage. I was me—the same me who was married, and had kids. Granted, I didn't remember having four kids. I couldn't remember their names, or birth dates. I didn't have a clue how to brush my teeth, or shave my legs. I didn't know how to read, but no, I didn't have brain damage. No way!

My occupational therapy was trying desperately to get me to focus on the past and the present, and though I was in denial about my brain injury, I knew *something* was wrong, and I was willing to learn. They started gradually. From dressing myself, to using the bathroom, we did it one step at a time. A therapist taught me how to wash my hair and shave my armpits and legs. I got nicked a couple of times and she felt horrible. Then we had a lesson in brushing my teeth. The items just magically appeared. I accepted that at face value. Then we focused on the family members, then what time I should take my meds. Slowly but surely, they added more things to do. They drilled me so much on my kids' ages that, to this day, I am self-conscious when asked how old they are. And it doesn't help that they keep getting older!

I remember they put my schedule on a whiteboard, but I couldn't read it. It just looked like a bunch of scribbles. It didn't help that they put PT, ST, OT on the whiteboard. I had no idea what that meant. The nurse very condescendingly said, "Physical therapy, speech therapy, occupational therapy." I still had no clue what that meant. *Why did I need speech therapy? I could talk, as soon as they capped my trach.*

My mom came the next day and handed me my son's preschool newsletter, and I read it word for word. The speech therapist told me, "Wow, you couldn't do that yesterday." I was like a computer that had to be rebooted. Slowly things started to go online again. I was very much in the now. I couldn't tell you who I saw earlier in the day; I was living in the present.

I remember being frustrated by a particular task given to me. I needed to place these picture cards in order of how they happened. The first scene was a father leaving for work. I got it wrong. I forgot the card that had him grabbing his briefcase. The next scene I failed was cooking on the stove, shocker (I hate to cook). And then she finally gave me a scene for soccer. I knew I had this one. I placed all ten cards in order, and she said I did it wrong. There was a slide tackle and I put it before the boy scored the goal. I defended my stance and she gave it to me.

I remember asking "why" to everything. They did not like that and were exasperated by all my questioning.

The first time the kids came to visit, they all came at the same time. I was so overwhelmed. They made so much noise, were loud, hanging on me, wanted to kiss me, and I shut down. I couldn't take it. Kyle saw this and immediately changed course. Then the next time it would only be Noah, then Isaiah, then Grace, and finally Anthony.

I remember Kyle brought Anthony to me, I kept calling him Noah. He pooped (shocker), and Kyle told me I needed to change him. He was so tiny, and I had no idea what to do. I couldn't even remember how to change a diaper, let alone a poopy one, and as for a five-pound baby, no way. He was so tiny, so fragile, I thought I was going to break him. Kyle walked me through it step by step; and later that morning, Anthony fell asleep on my chest.

I was heartbroken when they told me I couldn't nurse. I asked why, and the doctor said it was because of the Coumadin (a medication I take to thin my blood). I asked if there was another medicine that would be safe for the baby, and he told me, "Well, you didn't want shots, so we gave you pills instead."

I didn't have any memory of refusing shots. I didn't remember them even telling me that's what I needed to do to nurse. I felt less than a mother. I felt like I was robbing him of the most natural thing in the world. I felt like I let him down, again. I remember a nurse coming into my room, and I was crying. I was devastated. She told me that she was getting information for me about the breastfeeding bank. In the back of my mind I didn't want a stranger's breast milk. I was thinking, *How am I going to bond with this baby if we don't get skin to skin, or comfort him through nursing?* I felt like I failed as a mother. This is the first time I really and truly failed at something that was so important and crucial, and I failed.

My record button wasn't on, which led to several heated discussions. I wasn't happy at the place where I was. I had a new physical therapist every day who didn't bother to read my chart. So when I did chest lifts, without a family member there, I was dying that evening and had no idea why. My daddy gave me a pillow to hug to try and relieve some of the pain. And it, of course, was at night, so there was no doctor available to prescribe medicine. At least that was my understanding. I didn't know that I had open heart surgery. I didn't know it was dangerous for me to do those exercises.

After that incident I realize that someone was always with me for my sessions and everywhere I went. When I went to PT (physical therapy), I had someone there. OT (occupational therapy)...someone was there, breakfast group...someone was there. ST (speech therapy)... someone was there.

I also was told to put on bright yellow socks because I was required to. I found out from Kyle it was a sign that I was a "fall risk." "When the hell did I fall, and why do I have to wear these things?" I was furious! People were already starting to look at me and stare. Now there was another reason to glare. Later in the month, they started to plug me into the wheelchair and my bed. To let them know if I was in danger of falling. I thought it was laziness on their part. Every time I gave someone a hug, I set off the damn alarm; and in my bed, I couldn't roll over. Nighttime was the worst. The night staff was horrible. They would sit at the nurses' desk and gossip all night. I would call for them and they kept telling me to use the button, but I didn't have the strength to hit it. I hated evenings. I had insomnia, which made it worse. And when they said they wanted to keep me for another week, I refused.

Gradually things started to improve. I was walking without any assistance, but then they put me in a walker. They said it was safer. I didn't question them because they were the doctors. I eventually got my right hand to work, sort of. I was still using my left to eat and write with, but the right hand was a little stronger. I stopped counting the number of times I removed the marbles from the clay, or moved the cotton balls from one bowl to the next, using my right hand. And those damn coins—I had to pick them up off the table and place them in a container. I got so frustrated, I picked it up with my left hand and said, "I'm done!"

For my speech therapy, I had a journal with everyone's

name and birth dates. When they asked me the date, I said it was 2001. The therapist wanted to know what happened that year, and my mom told her that I got married that year. "Oh, that makes sense." And that's all I remember that she said.

For OT, I had to go to breakfast group. It consisted of the four of us eating together. Thickened liquids were required, and were disgusting, except for the chocolate milk. It was like a milkshake. There was one gentleman who was refusing to eat. The teacher in me came out, and I started to encourage him. We would eat our oatmeal together. A couple weeks into it, his daughter came to my room to let me know he was going back to the hospital, but wanted to thank me for being so kind to him. I was just being myself.

It was during this morning breakfast that I got to choose a soda. What did I want? The only name I could think of was Coke. It was the best-tasting Coke EVER! I didn't even think it was weird that I was having Coke for breakfast. In my former life, that was a huge no-no. It wasn't even an option. A couple of days later, they wouldn't let me have it because they said I aspirated. *When did that happen?* I had no memory of it.

And they wouldn't tell me, either. I felt like a child, and no one would talk directly to me. I was a capable human being, responsible for thirty students, and my four babies. Why wasn't I being talked to? Why was I in an eating group, being taught how to eat again? Why did they keep telling me to close my airway when I swallowed? How in the world was I supposed to do that?

After several weeks at the rehab hospital, I finally did go home, and I realized that I couldn't handle it. The kids were really loud—I mean really loud. I had spent more than two months in a hospital and rehab, with a very quiet room, and came home to loud noises everywhere. I wanted to crawl into a hole. And there were a lot of people in my house. Beyond that, my house didn't look like my house. We had new floors, new baseboards, bookshelves with containers in them. My quilt was gone. Katie and Andrew moved in, the three kids were sharing a room, and my California king-size bed was now a queen. I cried for three days. All my memories of my house from before were gone. It was a good change, don't get me wrong, but I couldn't remember choosing the new floor, or telling them to take down my quilt. I had absolutely no memory of any of it. It frightened me, and everyone was so happy with the changes, I figured that I needed to be, too. I hid in my room. I scared my kids. I frightened them with my language and my short temper. I said whatever I was feeling and didn't hold back. I swear I made everyone blush with my colorful language. Despite all of that, my family was my rock. They were with me constantly. I'm sure they thought I was crazy, but I didn't feel any judgments.

When the baby cried, I did nothing. I didn't even look at him. I didn't coo over him, or kiss him. I barely held him. I remember after I got home, I started a new intensive program called the CRC (Cognitive Recovery Center) at St. Jude Hospital. It was there that they taught me how to make his bottles, and change a doll's diaper. I told them, "This baby is a lot bigger than mine." They thought I was lying, I'm sure of it. They didn't know the history. I could barely tell them. I had to write out his schedule and make the bottles on the weekend.

Susan, my occupational therapist, very firmly, with love in her voice said, "He's your responsibility. You need to take care of him and hold him. He needs to feel you and smell you. He only has one mother, and you are it." She called me to greatness. She challenged me to be involved.

Later, I made Kyle bring him to pick me up and I showed him off with pride.

It was at the CRC that a therapist taught me that I could say no to any treatment I didn't want to do. That was, perhaps, some of the best therapy I received, because for once I felt empowered. I know their job is to get people back to their jobs, but it was obvious to everybody that teaching again would be out of the question. I couldn't add, let alone memorize, thirty kids' names. Despite that, I was assigned a task of teaching a lesson, but I didn't have my supplies, and what I had to work with were worksheets, not lesson material. And so I said I wouldn't be doing the lesson. Of course, the speech therapist that had assigned the task didn't work with me the day I was supposed to do it. I ended up with Nicki, a wonderful sweet speech therapist in training that day, and I felt bad that she had to be on the receiving end of my stubborn refusal, but I was sticking to it. I was finally taking control over my new life.

Lyle and Armando, my two physical therapists, gave me the skills to get back on my feet, literally! I started off in the wheelchair and left in a walker. Eventually I got to the cane and those two have been encouraging ever since, and still are (I see them in group therapy three times a week). They never gave up on me. Lyle was always positive, encouraging me, my cheerleading section, and Armando pushed me to tears. But I needed both of them. I needed the gentle touch and the kick in the pants. With their help, I was walking with a cane for a while. Unfortunately, I got sick with a virus last year. Since then, I have not been able to get out of the walker. My neurologist thinks the virus settled in my cerebellum, messing up my balance again.

It kills me that I am back in the walker, and I feel I am disappointing them. They worked so hard. And they did a great job, but setbacks are a part of my life now.

Physical and cognitive problems were not the only problems I faced. Mentally and emotionally, I needed a lot of help, too. I met with Dr. Colleen (a wonderful psychiatrist) at CRC and then continued to meet with her for an entire year. It was the best decision I made.

Most people didn't understand that, when I came out of my coma, I was not thankful. I was not happy. I was not grateful. I was pissed off. When people said, "Oh, the miracle is here, let me touch you," and "God is so good for bringing you back," I just felt rage. I thought, *Thanks a lot for bringing me back half-assed. A cripple who can't walk, can't run, and can't get down on the floor with my kids. Yea, thanks for that. Thanks for making everything so hard now.*

Nobody seemed to understand what I had lost. The physical limitations were just what people could see, but a brain injury can take so much more. I also lost the ability to empathize with people. I lost my patience. I lost my ability to teach. I lost my ability to remember names. I lost my basic math skills. I couldn't stand it when my own children touched me and wanted to get close to me.

With Colleen's help, I was able to focus on my anger, and talk through it, and get past my fears of my kids touching me. It took over a year, but I eventually found my feet again.

In July 2011, on the Alaskan Highway, I had my God moment. Kyle and I were driving along this beautiful, two-lane windy highway and it started to rain. There wasn't another car around for miles. The forest enveloped us on both sides. It was so green, with varieties of green everywhere, and plethora of trees. I rolled down my window to breathe in the fresh air. The sky was dark up ahead, the rain was coming down sideways, at an angle, and then right in front of us was a rainbow. The bow was on the road. It was perfectly shaped. As we drove through the rainbow, the color in the car changed ever so slightly. I held my breath as we entered it. It was then that God washed away all that anger. In an instant, it was gone. I wasn't angry, I forgave Him. I needed to forgive Him. I was free from all of it. I said that I was sorry, and what He said in return is for me only.

When we got home from Alaska, I signed up Isaiah for religious education, aka Faith Night, and I am back at church. We are going there three times a month, which is huge for me!

I also realized that I can't keep on worrying about disappointing other people. Being a walking miracle is a huge responsibility. I feel like I am disappointing hundreds of people when they see me in the wheelchair. In their minds, I should be healed. But in reality, my life is hard enough as it is. And I know when people say, "So, you're back in the wheelchair?," they mean to show concern. And I need to find the peace to not try to defend myself. The truth is that I might always need a wheelchair. I will probably use the shower bench for the rest of my life. I might be able to use my walking sticks again, or a cane in fact. I just don't know. And I can't beat myself up for the setbacks, because there will be setbacks. It's inevitable.

No one, I mean no one, knows the effects of ninety-five minutes without oxygen. It can't be explained. It baffles doctors and physical therapists. I am unique; I am by myself, trying to figure out what to do next. I have major setbacks. Last week, I dropped an entire tray of chicken nuggets on the floor and burnt my arm in the process. Two weeks before that, I fell in my kitchen as I tried to make lunch for my boys and talk on the phone to my friend. My feet and hands are going numb again, and I have no idea why. To this day, my temper rises quickly to the surface when I am tired, and a room full of people still overwhelms me. I have had to realize that I am not the same person I was.

Where I once did many tasks at once, I must now take it slowly, even if it means unloading the dishes for twenty minutes. It is frustrating, I won't lie. So I will rely on my humor, family, and friends to get me through this. But the alternative is death, and I am choosing life.

I choose to live. I choose to dream. I choose to raise my four beautiful children. I choose to be Kyle's partner. I choose to be a good sister, daughter, and friend. But most importantly, I choose to do God's work, however that plays out.

A NURSE'S PERSPECTIVE
BY MARY KAY BADER, RN

Brynn's survival, awakening, and return to life as a wife and mother are a MIRACLE. Her journey from death to life is filled with countless "God moments" but she is not the sole recipient of these experiences. Contemplating the sequence of events involving all the different individuals with their own unique skills and gifts brings us closer to understanding our purpose in this world. When we allow ourselves to be open to these moments, collectively we become part of the miracle.

As nurses, physicians, and administrators, we all have specific reasons for choosing our profession and work. Each of us has unique beliefs. For some who believe their work is an extension of God's ministry, the call to be part of something great may not be seen in the moment, but appreciated sometime after the event. As I was one of the many participants in Brynn's story, I truly believe we were privileged to be called in one way or another to help create Brynn's miracle.

The team at Anaheim Regional was called to be part of Brynn's journey. Joan Strydom was the charge nurse from the ICU who responded to the Code Blue when Brynn's heart stopped working. Joan's determination to keep the team working for ninety-five minutes, doing CPR, was exceptional, but it did not end there. She believed the hypothermia treatment was Brynn's only chance for recovery. Joan took that belief all the way up the administrative chain of command until she received the permission and support she needed. Dr. Eugene's skills and presence in the hospital at the exact time of Brynn's arrest were essential to her survival. April Pannozo, staff nurse and educator for the ICU, had been working on developing a hypothermia protocol for six months prior to Brynn's arrest. She telephoned me in June of 2009, asking for help in developing the protocol. I spent an hour on the phone with her that day, sharing knowledge and Mission Hospital protocol so she could develop a hypothermia protocol at Anaheim. The phone call led to a vital connection on the day of Brynn's arrest. Alison Legendre, the cardiovascular nursing director at Anaheim, reached out to her cousin, Kenn McFarland (CFO at Mission Hospital), on the evening of December 2, asking to borrow the hypothermia equipment Mission had—and Anaheim needed—to implement the hypothermia procedure.

The team at Mission Hospital was connected to Brynn in diverse ways. Kenn's immediate approval of allowing the Arctic Sun machine to be sent to Anaheim was a "God moment"! How many administrators would allow a fifty-thousand-dollar machine out the door without delay? If he had reacted cautiously or considered consulting the legal counsel to assure no risk was involved, the delay produced would have led to the absence of hypothermia treatment and Brynn's eventual brain death from the destructive chemical cascade that follows prolonged cardiac arrest.

My relationship with April opened a door between two hospitals. When I received the first call in the evening of December 2, my primary concern was for the patient and the nurses tasked with providing Brynn with a treatment that they had never been educated on, nor understood the complexity of care involved with delivering hypothermia. I took fourteen phone calls over the first thirty-six hours, and slept with my cell phone next to my bed in order to answer the calls throughout the night from April and her team. Every hour, we discussed the treatment protocol and how Brynn was reacting to the procedure. The team required guidance, and I was able to assist them in providing hypothermia safely and assuring it was therapeutic to Brynn. The calls continued for the first week. Teresa Wavra, another advance practice nurse from Mission, helped answer questions. She visited Brynn on the third day and helped the team identify the presence of seizures. Her collaboration with the ICU nurses led to consultation with neurology in order to manage the seizure activity. During the first week of Brynn's hospitalization, we were called to be part of her journey.

I did not hear from April for three weeks until a few days after Christmas in 2009. At the time, Brynn had been in the ICU for twenty-eight days. I didn't even know Brynn's real name because it was not shared with me over the phone. On December 30, April called me with excitement in her voice. Brynn had awakened from her coma and was speaking. April told me that Brynn got to see her baby. I smiled and asked her what the baby's name was. She answered, "Anthony." My breath caught as I could feel the tears forming in my eyes. I told her my father's name was Anthony. He had died in 2004. Both of my parents were "very Catholic" as Kyle would describe them and served God and others during their lives. My mom had died in 1993.

Then April said, "Brynn's daughter visited, too!"

I asked April, "What was her name?" She answered, "Grace." The tears fell down my cheeks as I experienced my "God moment" for my mother's name was Grace. I considered the events that had occurred over the past month and knew somehow my parents and I were part of something very special.

Kyle's journey during Brynn and Anthony's hospitalizations was shared with us in this book. His deep love for

Brynn and his family was evident on every page. It was his open, honest, and challenging relationship with God that brings focus to the heart of this story. Kyle experienced the revelation that it is when you open yourself completely to God and believe in the impossible...that something like a force or Spirit fills the void and brings life. The heroes, blessings, and God moments shape the miracle of Brynn's recovery. As Kyle says so eloquently, "God gets the credit for all of it."

EPILOGUE

Our story does not end here. Our story continues, and will continue for what I hope will be many, many years. Nothing illustrates that better than the Christmas letter from 2009. Much of that letter was a condensed version of what you've just read, so I've left you with just the end—an end that is, for the Ervin family, a new beginning.

Ervin Family Year-End Letter, 2009, continued...

As I sit here and write, this miracle is still unfolding before me. Tonight I got to lie next to my wife in her hospital bed, and fall asleep while watching a movie. I look forward to doing that many more times throughout our lives together.

Okay—not that I want everybody to bawl their eyes out, but if you don't have at least a tear in your eye right now, you might want to consider "stone cold assassin" as your next career choice. I hear the money's good. That being said, I can't end this letter with a bunch of people crying, soooooo...

ON THE BRIGHTER SIDE, WE WILL START FROM YOUNGEST TO OLDEST...

Anthony is doing amazingly well. While at the NICU, he got the nickname Benjamin Button because he had absolutely zero fat, so his skin just hung on his skeleton and he had an uncanny resemblance to the "baby" in the movie. But my newest son is packing on the pounds like a Sumo wrestler prepping for a big competition. He's also figured out how to find his way into his old man's good graces by pooping for everybody but me. I swear I've only changed one poopy diaper since he's been home. That is nothing short of FABULOUS. His nickname now is Squeaky McSqueaks because he grunts and squeaks just about 24–7. Poor Aunty Katie is getting introduced to the realities of parenthood in an extraordinary fashion. I'm beginning to think she might be feeling a bit nostalgic for the ridiculous grind of trying to get a PhD in chemistry.

Noah, as I have been told by my mother ad nauseum, is the carbon copy of his old man at the same age. He is full of piss and vinegar and charming smiles. His old man (having played that game) doesn't fall for the charming smile quite so easily and so his favorite things to say to me are... "**You be nice a me! You be nice!**" And "**Meany!**" These exclamations usually follow an argument over whether he can wear his *Star Wars* underwear **AGAIN**. He just simply will not accept the fact that he cannot wear the same pair of underwear day in and day out. But overall, he is a very sweet boy and has taken on the BIG BROTHER role with open arms.

Isaiah is my sensitive shy guy. But boy does he come alive on the soccer field. I was amazed at how seriously he took his role. You see, His team was not very good (it was mostly four-year-olds whereas the other teams had many five-year-olds). I think they won one game all season. But Isaiah's defensive prowess, at the very least, kept the scores respectable. The pressure did get to him at one point though. At halftime of one game, he came off the field, his face bright red with exertion and said, "I'm tired of doing all the work!" I just had to smile. He's definitely got some of his old man's competitive nature.

From his mom, he got the ability to say just about anything with his eyebrows. The other day, he said to Holly, "You know, Nana, when boys see pretty girls, they do *this* with their eyes." And he raised both eyebrows up and down like the wolf in the Bugs Bunny cartoons...Friggen hilarious.

Grace has been fortunate enough to find an excellent program in the school she's at. The program is a K-3 combined class that she has been in since kindergarten. The first two years were great but it is becoming apparent in her third year just how special this program is. The teachers are nothing short of remarkable and she is thriving in the environment they provide. She will be playing the Goose that laid the Golden Egg in their upcoming class rendition of *Jack and the Beanstalk*. It is a singing part, and I can tell you with no small amount of fatherly pride that SHE KILLS IT!!!! I cannot wait for the recital. Beyond that, she has now learned to spell all the good cuss words. Growing up in our household, she may end up lacking decorum, but, by God, she won't be illiterate!

On a down note, Crookshanks (the bane of field mice everywhere), perhaps sensing the unfolding tragedy in our family, ran away the night of Brynn's embolism. Unfortunately, we did not even realize he was missing until several days later. We think he may have been hit by a car but cannot be sure. Bingo mopes around the house looking for his feline friend and we all miss him terribly. He was a great cat.

As for me...I'm tired of writing, so I'll just say... I've been incredibly blessed. Few people get the opportunity to learn just how loved they are. Brynn and I have now had the opportunity (though neither of us would have wished for it) only to find that we are loved beyond measure. The outpouring of support has been tremendous, and we are so thankful.

So I end this year with a mighty thank you... thank you for your prayers, thank you for your help, thank you for all that you have done to help me and mine get through a most trying time. We love you.

The Ervins
Brynn, Kyle, Grace, Isaiah, Noah, Anthony, and Bingo

ACKNOWLEDGMENTS

First, I thank my wife for continually providing me with the encouragement and focus (and the occasional kick in the pants) that she knew I required to finish this book.

Second, I thank my children for always going out to play in the backyard whenever Daddy was writing.

Finally, I thank my friends and family who, with great patience, read every iteration of this book that I threw at them. You were always generous in your praise and gentle in your attempts to direct me to telling a better story.

ABOUT THE AUTHOR

Kyle Derek Ervin is a husband and father of four. He studied English with an emphasis in creative writing at San Diego State University and received his bachelor's degree in English from California State University Hayward. While in college, on a whim, he joined the United States Marine Corps. There, he served as a reservist in the 4th Light Armored Reconnaissance Battalion. Kyle was raised in San Jose, California, but now lives in Fullerton, California, where he works for Vironex, Inc. as an advanced characterization specialist. This is his first book.

Cerise,
   I am so glad I
was placed at Sierra
usta! You have been a true
friend!
         I love you!
              ♡
            Brynn